# JACKIE BIBBY

## The Texas Snake Man

**A Very Nice and Kind...** *Gentleman*

By Jackie Bibby

# Dedication

The Bibby Boys—Michael and Matthew!

The Grands!

Alexander, Annabell, and Donovan!

Jackie Monoa Bibby!

# About the Author

Jackie Bibby—handling snakes for over fifty years

Now, let's dive into what has defined so much of my life. Handling rattlesnakes is what very few people would ever consider doing, yet I've spent upwards of five decades doing just that. I have been dealing with them for over fifty years, developing skills that most people wouldn't believe possible.

For over thirty-five years now, I have been deep into the field of addiction recovery, working to help people fight their demons just as I have had to fight mine. It has been work that shaped my and many others' lives whom I crossed along the way.

In the process, I experienced a journey that took me to places I never thought I would visit. I've been incredibly fortunate to have had the opportunity to appear in scores of feature films and made-for-television movies. If you're a television buff, perhaps you've seen me in an episode or two of many shows that have aired over the years.

For three seasons, I was the lead character in Animal Planet's *Rattlesnake Republic*, sharing my world with a viewership who probably hadn't even seen a rattlesnake up close, much less handled one the way I do.

My story did not end there. I starred in two documentaries that looked intensely at me, my life, and this remarkable world in which I live. It was in those films that I could share much more about myself than just my skill with rattlesnakes, a window into the outside world about the complexities of my life, handling snakes, managing addiction recovery programs, and balancing the personal challenges that go hand in hand with living such a public life.

Now, if you are interested, you can find over forty videos on my official YouTube account.

To me, each of them is a little share of my legacy—a view into a life not like any other.

Even with thoughts of my past, I simply cannot help but think about the present and the future. I'm in my early seventies now. Still active. Still out there, still hitting new challenges as hard as I can. Far from retirement.

Running a nonprofit foundation that I hold very close to my heart—***ROATCH Foundation***—going on with live shows, and continuing to spread awareness about both the dangers and beauty of rattlesnakes. It's a calling, I suppose, something that really never lets go of you.

Even to this day, years later, I find myself returning to the pit to face off with the creations that have been a part of my story.

But that's not all. I balance many film and video projects at any given time, and from time to time, you may find me popping up on one of the big-name podcasts out there. It's opened up another way that I can share my story, reach new audiences, and speak with people who may not have otherwise known my work. It is just incredible to think that at this point in my life, I am still learning, still growing, and still doing what I love. There's no slowing down yet.

Now, even if I may have crossed over to my seventies, I am far from done. By any stretch of the imagination, there is so much more that I want to do, more stories I want to tell, and more lives I want to touch.

Far from it being the end of the line for me—*it's just another chapter.*

# Contents

# Prologue

If I may modestly submit, this is my story. I have tried my best to be as truthful as possible throughout. There may be things that I might have missed and maybe even some people whom I should have mentioned but did not.

Life is just like that sometimes; there are moments that you would like to remember, but then somehow, they slide away, and there are people who have entered your life—people who have touched your soul, who deserve mention, but in the whirlwind of experiences, their names might not make it to the final page, the final chapter.

But know that if I have left any part of my story out, it was not intentional.

I have indeed lived a life full of adventure, risks, and, yes, even blessings. It has been a meandering journey full of unwelcome twists with innumerable challenges, yet I have remained perseverant.

Looking back, every single struggle seems to have mapped a road to better things and a purpose I have not always known or envisioned but which was shaping me all the same.

My life, surely, has not been easy at all, but it is uniquely mine, and I wouldn't trade it for anything.

If you've picked up this book and followed me through my stories, then I believe you've come to know me better than most people ever will. You've seen my highs, my lows, my successes, and my failures.

Into these very words, I have tried to put as much openness as I can—to let you hear my voice, feel the weight of my thoughts, and understand the kind of man I have grown to become over the years. Hopefully, you have found it interesting, at times even inspiring.

*After all, this journey of mine has not been anything but dull!*

# Chapter One

# The Attention Seeker

I always knew I was special. I knew I'd be known and recognized. Hell, I knew I was going to be a star. I was wild and notorious, and maybe that's the Texan way. Something of a daredevil ran tight in my blood, passed through generations.

However, I always felt strongly that it was all written in the stars for me. It was destiny that I'd live a life of adventure, of pure drama and danger.

I was born in Grand Prairie, Texas, on December 20th, 1950. I was in Grand Prairie because my grandparents lived there. They worked for Ling-Temco-Vought (LTV), a conglomerate that existed until 2000.

They made almost anything, including aerospace, airlines, electronics, steel manufacturing, you name it. At that time, my father was working in the oil field, so he was traveling a lot.

So, when my mother was carrying me, her first child, she was living with her parents in Grand Prairie. I was told that after the delivery, my grandmother was in the delivery room with my mama, and upon seeing me, her world turned upside down.

She almost dropped on her weak old knees and perhaps shed some tears. My grandmother was absolutely terrified, and you wouldn't blame her either if you saw what she witnessed. I was faceless, the first baby in history to be born without a face.

She wondered how miraculous it was that I was still alive, and then the Doctor went on to say that I sure was a lucky baby. It was no surprise to Grandma that I was lucky, but still, you don't call a faceless kid lucky? Now, do ya?

Anyway, the doctor did clarify. Sure, I am nothing short of a miracle, but I was born with that pretty face. I just happened to have a portion of the placenta attached to my forehead and draped over my face. It's not a terribly uncommon thing, but it's relatively rare. It's called being born with a veil.

Well, that's when everything was planned out for me, right at the moment of birth. Whatever I did, I'd do to ensure I got my fair share of attention. The doctor had to get scissors and snip the veil away. But before he could snip the veil away, I was already trying to breathe.

They didn't even have to spank me to get me to breathe. I'm guessing I was in a big hurry to get into this world.

When I turned two, our family moved to Rising Star. My father agreed to buy a house from one of his aunts. The house was right across the street from hers, and thus, we were in a little house at 211 East College, Rising Star, Texas. Rising Star became my life. It witnessed everything I did for the first time, and it helped me to become the man I am today.

If I recall the first mischievous activity I took part in, it'd be around 1955. I suppose I was four or five, and I stole my grandfather's car. Back then my grandpa used to let me sit around in his lap and drive. I'd take control of the steering wheel while he would look after the pedals.

I was a kid, so my feet could never reach the pedal. This was before school started. One day, my Papa came over while our family, Mama, and Daddy, were out on the porch. He got out of his truck and began talking with my daddy and I think he intended to keep the conversation short because, as I saw it, he left the truck running.

The little devil whispered in my ear, *'Get on that car.'* And so I did.

It was an automatic car, so I got in and pulled it in gear, and off I went to my little adventure. I couldn't even see over the steering wheel, but I drove off anyway until Papa and Daddy noticed me. And what next? They both chased me across the street until they caught up to me. Good for me, they weren't even mad, and they sure had a good laugh about it.

My sister, Velda Dean Bibby, was born on November 15th, 1952. With her birth, we became a family of four. It was an unspoken tradition to have small families. My mother had one brother, and my father was an only child. So, we, too, were a small family with very few family members. Velda was almost exactly two years younger than me. My mother told me a story about when Velda was born.

I was a curious little kid, and when she was born, in the weeks that followed, I'd always see her wrapped in a piece of cloth. She was the shape of a nugget, and all I could see was her face. I had never before seen such a small baby, even though I myself was almost a baby, but anyway, I'd stare at my baby sister all the time.

One day, my mother came into the room to check up on her, and I was there with her. I had pushed a chair up beside Velda's bassinet, uncovered her, and picked her up by her feet. When Mom saw me, I was holding her by her feet, and I told her, "Look, mama, she got feet."

You can't blame me; I was curious. It'd been months since she was born, and not once did I get to see her feet. I think this was the first indication that I had something going on with the feet, a foot fetish of some kind.

Either way, years later, karma did get me, and I lost my right foot. This is who I am. I really don't know when to stop, and also, quite interestingly, I don't think I can tell anything between safe and danger. For me, it's all a blurred line. You see, you don't get called Texas Snake Man for pulling improvised shows. Me? I go all out, get dumb, and get a living.

Speaking of dumb, I started school early, which didn't make sense to me. They had a program where my parents put in extra money so I could begin school early, and it was weird because we didn't even have kindergarten back then. They were just from Grade One till Grade Twelve. I was enrolled in school for the first grade when poor me was just five years old, which made me the youngest in my class.

When I first started in the 1st grade, I was in a class of twenty-five students, and by the time I was in 12th grade, there were twenty-seven students, and of these, only eleven were the kids that were together with me in the 1st grade.

Beating around the bush, I simply did not fancy the idea of attending school at such a young age. Besides, I did not like school, and if that wasn't doing the charm, I was a mama's boy.

My daddy was never around much due to his work duties, so I was pretty drawn to staying with my mama. I detested the thought of leaving my mother for even a minute. Against my wishes, my folks put me in school, and me being the rascal I was, I prepared my own plans.

Whenever I would get the chance, and this was usually the teacher not paying attention to me, I would sneak out of the classroom and head straight home to my mother.

I don't understand why, but rather than appreciating the thought, she would take me back to school. If that doesn't tell you how obedient and well-mannered of a boy I was, then I don't know what will. If it were some other boy, he'd run off to some adventures, causing trouble. Not me. Anyway, on this day, we lined up in lines to go inside the classrooms to our designated seats. As we were lining up I looked around and found the teacher not paying any attention to me. Here, the little daredevil whispered again, *'Take your chance, buckaroo.'*

And so I did. I stuck out the line and took off down the road and headed straight to Sweet Home to my lonely mama. Well, as I said, today didn't have it for me because, for whatever reason, the principal came out for an inspection.

On his rare occurrence of inspection, my strolling caught his attention, and he decided, *'Why not leave school and my duties and chase this little boy?'*

He followed me down with the intention of bringing me back to school. About a block and a half away, I noticed him coming after me, and he was alarmingly getting close to me, so I scooted. I jumped off in a bar ditch under a bridge and ran down a creek bed. I was relieved and thought I had outrun him.

But our principal was quite a man. This guy followed me well and got really close. With no choice, I did what needed to be done. I picked up pebbles and hurled them at him, and

I continued until he went back to school and finally left me alone.

I was really proud of myself. I was successful on my mission as I went back home, and this was one of those rare days when she did not send me back to school; she just took me the next morning. The day was unusually different, and everyone was looking at me weirdly.

They looked very excited for a dull day. I went over to the kids and asked what was with the look, and they told me that it was unbelievably cool that I had thrown rocks at the principal.

This! This was the first time I was given attention without asking. Now, ever since I was born, I have been inviting attention, but this was the first time I was given attention from a multitude. And I loved it. Seeking attention was the bedrock of my life. It was in the first grade that I got in on my first-ever fistfight. It was with a boy named Jimmy Kendrick.

Forgive my memory, for I don't remember what led to the vicious and deadliest brawl, but what I do remember is Jimmy chasing me, and I took off running into the soccer field, which was a junior high soccer field.

Now, we little kids never went out on that soccer field. It was just off-limits for us. There, Jimmy finally caught me, and he had me down and gave me a good whooping of my life. To our surprise, the older boys were there because it was our recess time.

Seeing us fighting was calling fun to them, so they gathered around us, and when they did, both Jimmy and I got scared. We knew what was coming.

Then and there, the two of us called a truce and scrambled back to where the first graders were supposed to be. It was way later down the road when I revealed the truth that I got my ass whooped. Before that, I told everyone that I was doing the whooping. I wanted attention, sure, but not the kind where I was getting made fun of.

My next fight was when I was in third grade. It was with this boy named Kenneth Rutledge. Now, Keneth was held back a year. He was a year older than the kids that were in the third grade, but since I got in school a year earlier, so, he was two years older than I.

Keneth was somewhat of an easy-going guy. Unlike me, who loved playing, he wasn't that into sports at all, and he was really slow. We were playing softball in the softball field one day, and I just was feeling a little mischievous that day, given that Keneth seemed like such a pushover, I thought, why not have some fun with him and give him some whipping?

Well, boy, I was wrong cause this guy whooped me well. Matter of fact, he gave me a horrible whooping. It was so bad it reminded me of Pops back home. But the day I lost some of my dignity, I gained a very good friend. Kenneth and I became really close friends after that, and we still are to this day. This guy paid to have a mural of me painted on his building. Keneth has a building downtown on which there is my mural, which says, *'Welcome to Rising Star, Texas. Hometown of Jackie Bibby, the Texas Snake Man.'* It's a picture of me with rattlesnakes in my mouth. Ain't that cool?

As I said, I loved playing sports. As a kid, I adamantly played football from fifth grade to the 12th I played all of the football. I almost missed two, and one of them happened on the football bus. We were on our way to the football game in high school.

When I was a junior, I was a starting center. And one of the things I really enjoyed doing and was keenly good at was telling jokes. So why should today be any different I thought that day. I started cracking jokes on the bus, and everyone began laughing to the point the coach found it irritating, so he told us to shut up. And us being obedient kids, we complied, but only for a mere minutes.

I couldn't resist, so as a few minutes passed by, I cracked another joke, and the bus began roaring with laughter. The coach wasn't having it, so he asked me to come up to the front and sit with him. On his account, I was being unruly, and I didn't agree with him, so I refused.

I agree, I did hurt his ego in front of the kids, but he didn't have to take my equipment from me. We were playing an out-of-town, it was an important game that I wouldn't want to miss. After all, my whole family was going to attend the game. And as if his taking my equipment wasn't enough, he took my jersey and said, "You're not playing tonight's game, boy."

I understand his frustration, but that was him taking it too far. I was incredibly upset, and everybody was dressing up for the game in the dressing room while I stood outside near the bus. Finally, my parents, along with Velda. With no choice, I went up to Daddy and told him about what happened.

He didn't say much to me and pulled the coach aside. I have no idea what my old man told the coach, but the coach came back with my equipment, and I was told that I'd be suiting up and playing the game.

Truth be told, my father had quite a reputation, a different one, to say the least. He whipped several of the teachers when my sister and I were in school. And just so I am clear, by whipping, I mean he physically whipped them because he didn't like what they were doing to his kids.

What can I say? He was very protective of us in his own way. But he was scary, I'll tell you that. The man could fight. He was one hell of a fighter. I don't know if he threatened him with whooping or sweet-talked him into it. Though I know he didn't sweet-talk. Still, I like the idea of him sweet-talking.

Either way, it worked. I got my jersey back but as fate had it, my football shoes were nowhere to be found in the equipment. Some greedy bastard stole them, but a good friend of mine had my back. David Harris, may he rest well in heaven, was a freshman, and his football shoes would fit just fine.

David took his shoes off, and he didn't play. He sat on the bench. But he had to go through the game barefoot before I would have football shoes to play in the game.

My father, throughout my life, took things into his own hands very frequently, and he successfully delivered, too. I never had to pay any price or any consequences for my actions.

And I hate to admit it, but I was really a spoiled child. Daddy was extremely hard on me, but he did make sure that no one else gave me much trouble.

At many points in my childhood, many tried to threaten me. And I'd always say this, "Do something to me. Come on, do something, and my dad will kill ya."

And it worked every time; they would stop bothering me because they knew damn well what my pops would do.

In life, I don't believe I truly lost something. If I did, I would always gain something. I also had a knack for acting, and my mom was influential in getting me my first-ever acting job.

Back then, it was really rare to have anything that you could play music out in the open.

You had to have a radio to play music. You had to have a record player. Well, my mother figured out a way to hook up a record player and some speakers in a pickup. We were having a parade, it was a yearly thing, and my first-ever role as an actor was playing Elvis Presley. I had naturally beautiful blonde hair, and for Elvis, she dyed my hair black. She painted sideburns on me and built me a microphone that stood up.

I had my own little stage in the back of a pickup. My mother and one of her friends drove the pickup, and we had a record player playing Hound Dog by Elvis, which I lip-synced for my performance, which was playing through these speakers that were on the pickup.

The girls at the back were supposed to be swooning and excited over Elvis playing the Hound Dog, but as it turned out, they were more enthralled by Santa Claus, who was floating behind them. They were paying more attention to Santa Claus than me.

What did I lose in this? My pride and ego and, above all, my attention. But I did gain my first ever acting experience, playing none other but Elvis Presley.

The tale of my childhood mischievousness is never-ending each year, not each month, each week, I'd pull some crazy stunt. My life took a drastic turn when I was eighteen. And it was solely because I was such an attention seeker. I got in the snakes because it was thrilling, exciting, and obviously life-threatening.

It was no different than flying airplanes, doing hang gliders, sky diving, scuba diving, water skiing, or even roller skating. It's fun, but it can kill you. I had my father's spirit, I did everything, and whatever I did, I was good at it. I was a good athlete and was always in great shape; you name it, and I would do it.

For me, the thrill in life was doing something fun and exciting.

When I saw that there was a Rattle Snake Competition Sacking Championship in 1969 at a roundup, I just couldn't let go. It was twenty-five miles away in Brownwood, Texas. It was literally calling me and how hard could it be? I just had to be myself, and I'd be good to go. Never in my life had I ever touched a rattlesnake before, and when I reached there, I was the only non-professional snake handler there; the rest came from their prestigious snake clubs.

I got in, they taught me how to hand a snake, and within a few minutes, I was all ready to rock and roll, cowboy style.

That was it, the start of it all, the life worth celebrating, my tears, joys, sorrow, pain, and pride. It was as if it was written in the stars for me.

From there on, I did what I liked, and I damn well enjoyed it. I lived it. As decades went by, I felt as young as I did when I was a boy.

# Chapter Two

# Thirty Dollars, Two Trophies, and My Name in the Paper

I was hungry, and I was clueless; I sought a thrill, but I didn't know whether I would get one. I could do a couple of things, but I couldn't put a finger on what I happily do. Surely, to get by, I'd work on a farm or get myself a business, a shop like my daddy did, but something in my heart told me about getting freedom by doing something I truly did. Now, I don't know what I loved, but I knew enough if it got me excited, I loved it.

And when I was seventeen, I pretty much heard my calling, and there was no denying it. There was a snake sacking competition here in Brownwood, Texas. You get to be handling snakes and play with them while the audience watches that you had me sold.

So, I went on and put myself up for enrollment, but I was told I was too young for this, and they had me rejected. In the end, against my wishes, I became the audience. I watched the guy handle those rattlesnakes and dance around its hisses, and I wished that was me.

But my eyes were set; I finally found something thrill-seeking; the simple thought of it pumped my blood. It was an adrenaline-producing sport, so in 1969, when I was eighteen, old enough to be around rattlesnakes, I successfully got myself in for the competition.

In my dreams of seeking a thrill, I never realized that you gotta need to know what you are doing so you can seek that thrill; there is nothing like you will learn to fly a plane when you start flying one; you have to have an education, years of it actually.

When I got there, I knew nothing about rattlesnakes, but I was a responsible man. I won't fly a plane hoping I would figure it out. I got my ten minutes of education before I went there.

Now, a lot would say that a ten-minute education was too little, and I was being careless, but I wouldn't have done wrong and not paid my part in destiny if I had not won that competition. I was a first-timer with no known knowledge of rattlesnakes or any snake in general.

All I knew was that they should not be trusted; they can kill you, and they hiss. Yet, I went in there and checked out with a $30 dollar prize money, two trophies, my name on the paper, and my hunger satisfied with my thrill and adventure. It was then I realized what the universe was calling me to, and I wasn't gonna ignore that call. It was no pride; I am a humble man, and I will prove it to you from the humbling experiences I had in my life, but I also was aware that my braveness, or what some called stupidity, was not something everyone was gifted with.

The rattlesnake sack competition was organized by a club named 'Venomairs' out in Fort Worth, Texas. In the first year in which I participated, the president of the club was Chuck Blythe, and in the second year, the president was Steve McBride. These guys knew what they were doing. They were professional handlers and knew everything.

They had medics, guides, and entertainers all lined up, making it the best show in town. In my first year, my partner, which was the guy who was holding my sack, was a good friend of mine, Dick Clark. He was real good with that and held no fear of snakes, but for the second year, it was Willie Ezzell who partnered up with me.

Willie wasn't as fond of snakes as Dick, but he did a good job of his fears, I still had to chase him down to get the snakes in the sacks, but I was proud of him. Help is a help, after all.

The $30 was just a sweet beginning of my victory, and I ain't speaking for the money here. I am talking about winning. For the next thirty or forty years that went by, not one year went by where I didn't win. Every year, I'd bring with me a shiny trophy, or usually several and after stacking a pile of them, I got my name in the Guinness Book of World Records.

In the first competition, in 1969, my time was around two minutes and eleven seconds. How this works is that you have two people with you. A pinner and a sacker, a pinner is the one who picks the snake and puts it in the sack.

The snakes that you draw are completely random, you don't know if that snake will be paying you any mercy or will be the realization of your worst nightmare. The sacker, your partner, tells you where the snakes are.

One wrong move and you will get your sweet kisses, which are anything but sweet. Now, my 1969 record meant that It took two minutes and 11 seconds to put all the snakes in the sack. In 1999, I moved to the Guinness World Record time of just 17.11 seconds.

In thirty years, I made quite a record. I am one of the two people on God's good green Earth who has sacked ten snakes in under twenty seconds.

There is one kicker: if you don't pin the snake properly or your luck runs out and you get bit, then you are gifted a five-second penalty.

Unfortunately, everyone makes mistakes, and I ain't no angel. I have been rewarded with the five-second penalty, but did it disappoint me? Absolutely not.

One time, I got that penalty, and I still managed to win the contest. It was crazy that even with the penalty, I was faster than everybody else. It was the first time I ever received a trophy and the prize money in the hospital.

I was pretty lucky at that; I was playing a dangerous game. The rules are simple: To get something, you gotta give something too. Risking isn't enough. I spent several years, ever since the first competition, without ever receiving a bite. But my luck soon ran out.

On my second contest, I was finally kissed by the sweet old snake, and I got it in none other than Brownwood, Texas, where I found my love for it. The snake bit me on my thumb, and that virgin bite put me in the hospital, where I spent eight days fighting a very high fever.

I remember on the third night in the hospital, I got blood poisoning from the snake, but it was not gifted from its venom. It was weird because it was an infection from its mouth, and I could see red streaks forming on my arm, reaching far up near my chest. Of course, my mother and daddy were there with me, and the doctor told them that if the infection got to my heart, I would die.

They gave me hot antibiotics and IVs that night, which stave off the infection from reaching my heart. It was pretty close but I survived that night.

When things got under control, and the threat of death loomed no longer in the room, my dad came to me. He worried. I could see the fear in his eyes as if he hadn't slept for days. I felt bad for worrying my daddy. He sat next to me and he pleaded and even begged for me to stop this.

He said, "Jackie, please don't do that anymore."

Although I was no longer in danger, I still was pretty sick and weak. But what I felt the most with intensity was guilt for making my family worried. It was horrible to see them like that, so I agreed to their pleas.

I told him sincerely, "I won't do it no more."

I meant it. I wouldn't want to worry my folks like that, and it was painful, too; it hurt really bad; my whole body was hurting. I was discharged and gained back my health, and weeks later, I was back doing it again. It was like a drug I almost OD'd on, and after making some honest promises, I relapsed and gave in to my desires. I was back at it, participating in rattlesnake roundups back in the pits.

When Pops found out that I was doing it again, you bet he was upset and started going at me.

He accused me that I lied to him. I understood what he was feeling, but I told him, "Daddy, I didn't really lie; I just changed my mind about it."

I was being honest. I couldn't go without doing that sport. I was so happy and excited about it. I felt it was made for me and believed that what I could do, no one else could. It felt like home. It felt personal. When I told my daddy that I was going to quit I wasn't calming him down. I intended to quit because those eight days were very horrible.

When you fell really ill and lay in bed with your fragile body, you dream about the days when you were healthy and running around. At that moment, you tell yourself that I will never drink ever again, I will never eat unhealthy food, nor will I ever sin. You do it because you miss being normal, and I felt the same. I wanted to feel normal, but as soon as I was normal, I just couldn't resist the adrenaline-pumping calling. So I just kept on doing it.

Now, that was a pretty horrible experience, but I wouldn't say I was afraid; I just felt uncomfortable in it. But that was just the beginning. In my career, I have had twelve snake bites that required Hospitalization. I only counted these because I had to go to the hospital for them.

Out of ten rattlesnake bites, four were what you call dry puncture wounds but with no envenomation. There was no envenomation because the rattlesnake had compressed its venom glands with muscle on the either to force the venom out through its fangs. It's like a hypodermic needle, just like when you press on the plunger. The striker has to compress his muscles on either side.

The snake can bite you and leave the puncture wounds, one or both fang holes. But there's no envenomation in a relatively short period of time. Those of us who've been bitten several times can tell if there's been an envenomation. Because if you've been envenomated there will be bruising, blood blisters, and dramatic swelling at the site of the bite. In all honesty, it's pretty ugly.

Those are all things it's going to be real readily noticeable, especially for somebody who's had a bad or seen a lot of bites. We'll know what they look like.

We can easily tell within thirty minutes if somebody needs to go to the hospital; if the coast seems clear, then we just wipe the blood off and go on about what we're doing.

There's a catch to this: it's not all ugly and painful. It is due to these snakes that I have traveled a lot. I've been to Europe sixteen times, all over the United States, with many trips to LA and New York for TV shows.

There was one time when I went to Holland. I made an appearance in a show called Kindid. It was a show with a live audience with live broadcasting. I was inside a sleeping bag, and I got a funny feeling of a rattlesnake in my pants.

I told my partner, Kim Garrett, *"I think I feel something touching my leg."*

Garret unzipped the bag, looked, and assured me everything was alright. He zipped it back, and a few moments later, I got that feeling again. I asked Garret again to take a hard look because I really felt a snake up in my pants. To make me feel comfortable, he unzipped again and looked properly. And sure enough, there was a little rattlesnake hanging out of my pants leg. This little one had crawled over my knee and up to my hip. He was a sneaky fella whose head was up against my hip.

Kim had no idea how to get him out of my pants, so he asked the people in the audience if they had a knife, and luckily, there was one guy carrying a pocket knife with him. Kim took that pocket knife from him and slit the hip of my pants open, and slowly took the rattlesnake out.

After that, he unzipped the sleeping bag, and we walked up to the show hostess and received applause from everyone on the show. They haven't had seen anything like and you could tell from the loud clapping they loved it. The truth was I never had anything like that either. It was funny because they thought we had done that on purpose, but it was not.

Another wild ride we had was several years back in the Oglesby rattlesnake roundup. I'm in the middle of a scene, sitting all calm-like in the pit area, with a whole heap of rattlesnakes slithering' around my feet. Now, we're there to show folks you can be as close as a prairie dog hole to these critters without gettin' bit, as long as you keep your wits about you.

Well, wouldn't you know it, one sneaky snake decided to hitch a ride up my prosthetic leg? Now, see, on that side, I can't feel a thing because of the prosthetic. So, there I am, oblivious as a hog in mud while this snake's making itself cozy up my britches.

Lucky for me, someone spotted the commotion and hauled that snake out faster than a jackrabbit on a hot day. We then went about our day. We thought about having something to eat, so we went into a café and ate then we went to convenience stores, going around, buying stuff.

So, there I am, back in the motel room with Dougie, getting comfortable after a long day's wrangling. I reckon it was time to swap out my fancy rattlesnake boots for something a bit more easy-goin'. I unzip my high-kneed boots, and what do I find? You guessed it, a rattlesnake cozying up in there like it was his own private saloon!

Now, let me tell you, I had been strutting around all day with that slithery critter in my boot, none the wiser. We'd been in cafes, convenience stores, the whole nine yards. If that snake had decided to make an appearance in public, well, it would've gone real ugly.

But luck was on my side that day because I only discovered our uninvited guest when I was back in the room, getting into my regular duds. When I saw that rattler, all bets were off—I chucked my boot across the room, and out he tumbled.

Now, picture this: me and Dougie, two grown men, hollering' like banshees at each other, "You get it, no, you get it!"

So, we called in reinforcements, and with some help, we managed to corral that snake into a beer box and took him back to the show the very next day. It was pretty funny, and we did prove our point unless enticed the snakes aren't dangerous.

There was one snake incident that had me nervously sweating, and it was about the time we took our show down to Brazil for a television special. We were in my hometown with the cameras rolling and were ready to put on a show like no other.

We called it **_Tattoos, Music, and Snakes._**

We had it all lined up—three tattoo artists setting up shop, musicians tuning their guitars, and us, of course, ready to wow the crowd with our snake show. Now, there were these two gals, both busy with their tattoo work. One of the girls was a really young girl, and both of them wanted to play with the snakes.

So, they came over to me and asked, "Got any snakes we can play with?"

Well, you know me, always ready to share the fun. People like them come over all the time who want to play with the snakes, and I always let them have their fun, but of course, with protocols, I point 'em over to this box where we kept a ball python, just a friendly little fella, nothing too rowdy. Off they go, like kids in a candy store, opening up boxes, looking for their scaly playmate.

One of them grabs what she thinks is a harmless flat rattlesnake and drapes it around her neck like it's a fancy necklace. Meanwhile, her friend got the right idea, wrapping a harmless snake around her own neck, just enjoying the thrill of it all.

The problem was, the first girl got her hands on one of the five-and-a-half-foot white rattlesnakes coiled around her neck, and she didn't even realize it was a venomous critter! When the crowd catches sight of this, you can bet there's some hollering' and carrying on.

Someone screams for me, and I come a-runnin', almost jumping out of my boots and straight to the two girls.

By the time I get over there, people are backing away like they've seen a ghost. And there she is, with a deadly rattler around her neck, as calm as a cat in a sunbeam.

I tell her real slow, "Take that snake off and lay it down gentle-like."

And she does just that, and I scoot on over, scoop up that rattlesnake without so much as a hiss.

That was a close call. She could've been bit, and things could've gone real bad, real quick. But it's like the good Lord above was watching out for her that day. And as for me, well, I reckon I aged a few years at that moment, but it was all worth it to see her safe and sound. If things had gone south, she would have been dead and I in prison.

If you have been out keeping your eye on TV, then there is a slight chance you may have caught a glimpse of me on TV. I have been in a fair share of TV shows and movies. After all, as I told you earlier, I set out with a snake in hand, but I also was aiming to be a TV star.

It all started back in the early '90s with the Chevy Chase Show. I had a really great and fun time with Chevy, where we talked about rattlesnakes. I chatted up with Jamie Lee Curtis and even bumped into the likes of Sam Elliott. But that was just the tip of the iceberg.

After that, I found myself mingling' with Jay Leno, shooting the breeze with Maury Povich, getting' real with Ricki Lake, and sharing stories with Sally Jessy Raphael.

And then there were the gigs like Walker, Texas Ranger, All Jacked Up, MTV senseless acts of video, and the Go Big Show. And let's not forget our very own Rattlesnake Republic, tearing up the airwaves for three whole seasons! I've had my fair share of appearances across the pond in Europe, too. All in all, I think that's a pretty impressive list for a country boy like myself. But there's always room for one more adventure.

One of the best experiences I have ever had with a celebrity had to be Snoop Dogg. We were doing a show down in Georgia, and we spent a good old month down there, and this was during the pandemic. It was a whole new ballgame with the COVID restrictions. We were holed up in this hotel like a bunch of hermit crabs, with nobody coming in or out except for the cast and crew.

That hotel might as well have had our names on the door because it was all ours, courtesy of the production company. We couldn't even step outside to grab a bite or run an errand. Nope, had to rely on the showrunners to fetch us whatever we needed, like we were royalty.

We were competing for $100,000 for the show. I didn't win, but I made it up for the finals, one of the funniest things that happened there, for which that experience stuck out to me. Snoop Dogg was quite a gentleman, and whenever we would meet, he'd call me Jackie Bibby Baby.

It sounded pretty cool when he said it, and funny too. And he would always fist bump me that was his way of greeting me. Snoop's love for jewelry was pretty obvious. He would wear real heavy jewelry on him all the time, from rings and watches to necklaces. One time, we met, and he fist-bumped me. I don't know what went wrong, but I started bleeding profusely. It was probably one of his rings that was too sharp, and it cut me.

There was blood on the floor, and medics rushed and tended to the cut I received, but I got real attention there and even laughed.

They all laughed and said, "You just came out of a pit full of rattlesnakes, and you didn't get a scratch, and you fist bumped Snoop, and you cut your hand."

It was fun and one rare thing to be called Jackie Bibby Baby by Snoop.

I've always felt like a performance artist at heart because when you're up there on stage or in front of a camera, you're stepping into another person's shoes, living another life. Now, there are a couple of projects I forgot to mention earlier that I'm mighty proud of. First off, there's this feature film called "Just a Little Bit Crazy." It's a real doozy of a flick, all about rattlesnake wrangling. I was one of the stars in that movie. You can find it on the internet nowadays, available for purchase.

Then there's this horror picture called "Party Girl." Talk about a spine-chiller! I played a part in that one where my face gets peeled off and slapped onto a lava lamp by some serial murderers. Now, I'll admit, watching that movie gives me goosebumps but I was fascinated at the same time. They had me all done up in makeup that looked so real, you'd swear I'd really lost my face.

They even slapped a prosthetic on there to make it look like my skin was getting peeled right off. Now, that's what I call some top-notch movie magic! I can't watch a horror flick without jumping out of my boots, but put me right in the thick of it on set, and I'm as happy as a hog in slop.

In my fun, my thrill, and ever-fulfilling life, I once paid a hefty price. It was the scariest moment of my life, right there in the heart of Dallas, Texas. I was putting on a corporate show in a grand hotel, with about three hundred spectators gathered around to watch. I was strutting about with a snake on a pinner showing it off to the crowd, when I got a mite too close to a big rattler.

He decided to take a bite right above my boot and sank his fangs into the top of my leg.

That snake hadn't had a meal in months, so he was chock-full of venom, and he unloaded the whole shebang right into my leg. They whisked me off to Parkland Hospital, one of the finest in the land, and I got there lickety-split within the hour.

The doctors and nurses worked their tails off for days, trying to save my leg. But three days after that bite, it became clear they had no choice but to amputate. They started below the knee, hopin' to salvage what they could, but the damage was just too severe. The tissue was all torn up, and the bone just wouldn't hold steady.

So, in the end, they had to take it above the knee, and that's where I wound up—above-the-knee amputee. After the dust settled from that ordeal, I was facing a whole new challenge for myself: a prosthetic that would let me keep on trucking like I used to.

There I am, trying to figure out how I'm gonna foot the bill for a new prosthetic, with companies left and right knocking at my door, trying to outbid each other for my business.

*"I'll do it for half price,"* says one.

*"I'll cut ya a deal,"* says another.

It was dollars flying every which way.

But I was blessed to cross paths with one of the finest fellas I have ever met, who goes by the name of Scott Williams. This here prosthetic wizard came into my life while I was still laid up in the hospital, and let me tell you, he was a real godsend. I didn't have insurance at the time, so every penny was gonna come outta my pocket. It was looking like a real headache trying to sort through all those offers.

Scott Williams, the man who became a guardian angel to me when I needed it most. Right before I was getting ready to leave the hospital, Scott strolled into my room and made me an offer I couldn't refuse.

He said, *"I'll give you lifetime benefits free of charge."*

Now, you can imagine my surprise and gratitude for such a generous offer.

Scott wasn't all talk, no sir. He backed up their words with actions. He built my first prosthetic leg for me, no strings attached, and took care of me like family for years to come. Now, back then, he was workin' for a company called Scott Savage Prosthetics. That outfit was a class act through and through. I owe them a debt of gratitude I can never repay.

When Scott left that company, there was no question in my mind. I was going with him because he was more than just my prosthetic guy. He was family. I know his wife, his kids, the people that he works with, Over the years, he's built me five different legs, each one better than the last, and he's always been there for me, no matter what.

One day, some no-good varmints decided to break into my house and make off with a few things. Now, you'd think they'd go for the usual stuff like jewelry or electronics, but nope, they had their eyes set on something downright peculiar—they stole one of my prosthetic legs! Can you believe that? Along with a Harley Davidson motorcycle from my museum, no less.

Now, that takes some real nerve.

Now, some of you might wonder, 'Why in tarnation would anyone steal a prosthetic leg?'

Well, those legs aren't just any old piece of equipment. They have computers in them, and on the black market, they fetch a pretty penny.

I have been asked many times, *"Was the pain of them snake bites worth it?"*

And every time, without hesitation, I tell them, *"Absolutely, yes."*

Now, I understand that the answer might not make sense to everyone, but to me, it's crystal clear.

This journey I've been on has been full of twists, turns, and the occasional buck-off. Sure, I've felt pain, more than my fair share at times, from them bites and the aftermath. But every bit of it has been worth it. I wouldn't trade this life of mine for all the gold in Fort Knox.

Sure, I ain't never been what you'd call rich, money-wise. But when it comes to feeling blessed and lucky, well, I hit the jackpot.

Every scrape, every scar, every snake bite—it's all led me right here, to this moment, feeling like the luckiest guy in the whole world. I've lived a life that's been packed to the brim with adventures with memories that'll last me a lifetime.

# Chapter Three

## The Folks on the Road!

You've had kids who grow to become engineers, some who set foot in the financing world; some become poets, some writers, and some do art as a profession. And that's the way of society; now, some choose a career they are good at, some are in it for the money, while some do it because they want to fit in. This had never been the case for me; I liked what was odd. And above all, I knew what I liked.

The worst thing that could happen to anyone is being stuck in the same place. People think it's the loss of a loved one, but it's not. It can never be. Death and loss are inevitable things. They break you and make you sad, but you live still. You are in a state of melancholia always, but you move on. So, despite the loss of a loved one, a person will mourn, and carrying remembrance in their heart, they will get up and move on no matter the pain and emptiness. Because the truth is, no one is going to help you.

As you have people who love, celebrate, and accept you, you still, with them, are alone. That loneliness with so many people around is a human experience. You reach a certain age where you are responsible for what you do. It means when you fall, no one's going to pick you up. When you hurt yourself, it gotta be you cleaning those wounds. So, from what I have lived, being stuck in the same place is every man's worst nightmare because you are the only one in control over it.

Not moving on, complaining, and not really living because you had to fit in. The loss of a loved one and the loss of money are all things that do not necessarily have you in control. How and when a person will die, you have no control, so you will never blame yourself for that. But years down the road, when you've lost your hair, and your body won't allow you to work anymore, you will eventually blame yourself for really not living.

It wasn't the profound love I had for snakes. I love snakes like I love any other animal, but what I loved the most, what drove me, was the fact that that platform was opening doors for me. Snakes were just a medium that made me feel fulfilled. They showed me my purpose in life.

They told me what I liked and they took me to places and to people I will forever hold close. I love the doors that they have opened because I use snakes as my hook. I use my experiences and things I've done like the Guinness records and the TV shows and the appearances in Europe. These things mattered to me. They gave me an identity. It's in the moments when I am out for an audition, and someone introduces me to someone with the Guinness World Records I made or my endeavors with snakes. That moment, I love that moment when their eyes pop open in surprise. I could read their minds when they think that's so cool, I can never do that.

They remember me for what I had done even though they do not love snakes or would never go near them, but regardless, there is respect and attention I receive that is profoundly beautiful and worth it all. And that's the key to anything that an actor has in his repertoire: to be remembered.

At 17, I had no big wisdom aspirations to get my purpose fulfilled. I didn't even know what my purpose was, but snakes became the vehicle. But when I began to recognize the mileage that I could get out of these things, I began to really milk it for all it was worth. You see if juggling bunny rabbits would have done it for me, then I'd be happily called The Texas Rabbit Man.

So, a guy like me who risks his life for the sake of fun and attention is sure to worry people. Although I feel bad for the worry I caused them for my adrenaline, I believe it was their worry that filled me with love. I just couldn't abandon my purpose because I didn't want to end up being stuck, but in exchange for all their worry, I was always careful with the snakes. Every time I'd go in a pit or a sack full of snakes, I wouldn't go there ready to die. I had every intention to come out alive.

People around me, those I adored, loved, and celebrated, I would, without thinking twice, take a bullet for them. Those people loved me and I had never had any doubt in my heart about that. Their feelings about me were certain, but some had mixed feelings about what I did.

Of course, when you are playing the game of death and every time you are with the snakes, you are seconds from your death, gambling your life away for the sake of fun, you definitely will cause some trouble for your loved ones.

I had some significant others who held the same spirit for the snakes as I did; they loved the adrenaline, the danger, the staking of life at the pit of snakes, and then I've had some who could not stand even ten meters from snakes. But it never mattered to me, after all, I was the different one. No one likes snakes. They cannot be trusted; they are venomous, and the hiss alone sends shivers down the spine. Their eyes, their skin, their silence, their crawling, their tongue, who wouldn't be scared of that? So, in a way, I always accepted people's fear of snakes and the worth of that fear.

Having said that, some significant others were snake handlers, too. One of my ex-wives, my third wife, Betty, number two. Betty had a real love for snakes, and we had, for what many would call the strangest, most dangerous wedding, we got married in a snake pit with three hundred snakes around our feet down in Laredo, Texas, in 1984. And yeah, it was kind of exciting.

It was filmed by a TV show called Real People. The funny thing was that the JUSTICE OF THE PEACE officiating the service did not stand next to us but outside of the pit where there were no snakes. And even out of that pit, just being around them scared him a lot. During our wedding, we had many snake handlers present at the wedding, and all were our friends. When we got to the center of the pile of snakes and began exchanging snakes, Betty accidentally dropped the ring.

And this was not a whoopsie thing. Betty was not clumsy but she had only three fingers on one hand as she lost them in a sacking competition where we both were competing. She was bitten badly and, in the end, had to have some of her fingers removed. She dropped the ring in the den of snakes, but luckily, we had Smokey Moore come to our aid.

Smokey was an established snake handler, the kind of guy I loved spending time with, and one of the old legends. So, thanks to him, he reached right down into that pile of snakes and snatched that ring right up, and we went ahead with the ceremony. We couldn't help but give our guests an improvised show for free at the wedding.

But everything went well, and Betty and I got matching tattoos on our chests, which were wedding rings with rattlesnakes inclined around them with our names and the date of our marriage. My name is first on hers, and her name is first on mine.

I told earlier how my father disapproved of my profession of handling snakes. I broke my promises to him, and I don't think he ever came to terms with this career of mine.

He respected what I did but I understand it was hard for him to understand what I wanted. With my mother it was pretty much the same. It wouldn't be a surprise.

After all, who would want their son to play with venomous snakes? But they wanted to support me, so two of them once attended a snake show in Brownwood to watch me perform. It is one of the greatest moments of life when your parents are there to watch you perform; it's a beautiful moment.

You always outperform yourself because you want to make them feel special. You want them to know that you aren't wasting your time but are good at what you do, and people love it, too. I had my fate handed to me differently because this was not football or baseball. It was another sacking competition where their son had to be inside with a bag of snakes. And my parents did not like it one bit. And after that they never attended another show.

But being my parents, they also wanted to know how it went, and they wanted to hear it from me, but the condition was simple: I had to call them after the show was over, not during the shows but after everything was done and dusted.

This was well before there were cell phones, so oftentimes, after a show, I'd have to stop at a pay phone and make a call to my mom. I could either call collect, she'd always accept it, or oftentimes, I had a calling card that I could use to make a long-distance phone call.

I suppose her condition of call was a way of making sure that I was as far from a snake as I could be. I knew when I was performing, she'd be home worried about me, and every time I would call her, it would be a relief to her.

But I was a lucky child, really privileged. I had my mom as my biggest supporter who supported me in everything I did, even in what she herself did not like. Now that I am seventy have children of my own, am a parent, and am burdened with responsibilities, I now realize how unappreciative I have been. Sure, they made mistakes, but despite that, I don't think I can ever repay their debt.

To love when you cannot love yourself, to support what you really don't yourself. It takes courage. But among these things that I now am grateful for, I also admire her creativity.

I am what I am because of her because as I know my mother she was the most creative individual I had ever known. She could do anything. She could paint. She could write. She could design. She made clothing. She made handbags. She made shirts. She made wedding cakes, she painted pictures, and she did all kinds of stuff.

So, my need to be a performance artist stemmed from her. Every creative thing I do is sort of a homage to her, her remembrance, and my gratitude to her. Her name was Felicia Elosia Sprayberry.

She was a hairdresser and ran a beauty shop most of her life. But she was also different than me. She enjoyed being in the company of others and liked to be by herself. She worked hard and took what she missed in socializing into her art.

She died in this place just outside of town that we owned. It was some hundred acres of land out there that we owned at the time. That was where she spent the last of her days and finally drew her last breath, leaving us behind for a better destination. She was real quiet, my mother. She raised some dogs and really enjoyed being in their company. She liked them so much that she would rather be with them, doing nothing than be with people.

But my mother also had a wild side. I would have to say that without a diagnosis, my mom was an alcoholic and an addict. She used to drink occasionally. She was a binge drinker. She didn't drink every day, but she also liked to take pills. It's a shard of glass piercing my heart; I understand the pain of being addicted. And her being her, she just succumbed to it and could never share her pain.

My sister, Velda Dean Bibby, was an angel in my life. My most precious treasure. My friend in one. Carrying the same blood, pain, and happiness as me. No one in anyone's family is closer than a sibling because they went through the same things as you. They can understand you better than anyone else because they know what you have been through. In God's honest truth, she was a diamond in the rough. And I am privileged person to have her as my sister.

She and I got along very well, although she is not an easy person. She is five foot tall, but don't let that fool you. She got some real guts in her. Velda can drive a cattle truck and a Harley Davidson, and she, too, like our mama, is a beautician. She ran a beauty shop for years and supervised many girls under her. Without a doubt, she is the toughest woman. No, she is one of the toughest people I know.

As I told you, I loved the spotlight, and loving a spotlight makes you blind. You don't know when to stop when it is too much. Luckily, I had her to humble me down. Growing I loved being in fights and I never knew when to stop. And no one could get me to stop, well, all but one, Velda. Whenever I was doing too much, my sister would jump in the scene with her little harmless trick that magically always seemed to work.

She would sneak up from behind me, wrap her arms around my neck, and choke me down. Whenever that would happen, I knew it was Velda; I'd calm down because that would be the only option I'd had.

Velda has been married three times, but what warms my heart to the fullest is her marriage to her current husband, Johnny Lee. It makes her brother happy and relieved that she married one of the greatest men because he makes her happy.

They are really close to me, a great part of my family. And their kids, Shane and Jory. They have done phenomenally well. They're doing really well financially, just great, outstanding citizens in their communities. My sister's been extremely blessed with a great husband and some great kids and all of them just support me to the highest degree. Throughout our lives, we always had Christmas at my mom's house.

Everybody in the family would come to my mom's house and have Christmas on Christmas Eve, and now that she is no more, the torch has been passed to Velda. And Velda is the one who knows how to organize a dinner. It's one of those weekends I look forward to the most. She hosts it every year in her house, and the whole family gathers there. To say the least, it's always a really cool event.

As I mentioned earlier, we have been part of a very small family, and not just us being a family of four. Our parents, too, came from a small family. My father was an only child, and my mother had one brother named C.L. Sprague Berry. C.L., as in Connie Lee, but for some reason, my uncle did not enjoy being referred to by that name. He preferred being called C.L. I suppose that made him sound so cool. C.L. is 15 years older than me, and ironically, we were the closest of friends. By the time I was 17, I was drinking almost every day. My uncle held some great liking for drinking, and that made us even closer.

With drinking as our driving force, we pulled a lot of shenanigans. Drinking is fun, but when you have some to drink with you, well, that's when real fun happens.

The two of us traveled many miles together, hitting the road, drinking, partying, and raising a cane. This one particular trip stands out vividly. Partially because I was amazed at how cunningly smart he was. He was shy but real funny too. We were both in a business where we managed a successful manufacturing plant.

We had a total of fifty-one employees so we were doing pretty good. My uncle had roots in the sewing industry, thanks to our grandparents, who kick-started our family's journey in that field. So, when we heard about a business training symposium in Austin, Texas, we jumped at the chance to learn how to be better businessmen and do a better job.

At the symposium, we were like eager students, soaking up every piece of advice and insight. I was the vice president and production manager of our family's company, while C.L. held similar roles in his own company.

We showed up, got ourselves signed up, and got our nameplates and workshop books. It was a three-day session.

And the moment the first break hit, we bolted out of there like a pair of wild horses. Austin became our playground. We tore through the city, unstoppable and untamed.

My uncle and I did what we did the best when we were together, we drank. We drank from place to place; we traveled to every bar we could find. And across the road, we came across many strip clubs, and they called to us. Who were we to say no?

But before going in, my uncle stopped by a convenience store. I didn't question whether I knew what it was for, but then I saw this guy grabbing notebooks. It was strange he was drunk before he even got there. Inside, he had me talking because as smart as he was, he too was shy like my mother, so it was me usually doing the talking.

But we were having the strangest most conversations with them which justified us grabbing notebooks from the convenience store.

We told these strippers that we were two freelance writers for a men's magazine and are currently working on a story between exotic dancers in the South versus the exotic dancers in the North.

It was a genius idea he had ever come up with because we were interviewing all these girls. We were jotting down gibberish. Most of the time, it was me doodling on the notebook, pretending I was deep in it. But it was amazing the attention we were getting from these girls.

Usually, strippers are just doing their jobs; they won't let you fool around or talk more than necessary, but we had VIP passes to everything. Every girl wanted to share her two cents, and we listened well. From club to club, we received the best experience one can ask for, all credit to C.L.

My life's memorable adventures didn't come only from my immediate family members but also from my extended family, or what I like to call them—the snake handlers. There are five of us, including myself, who've been wrangling snakes together for over four decades.

These guys are more than just friends; they're like brothers. I know their wives, their marital histories, their kids, and even their grandkids. The five of us have traveled the world together and formed a beautiful bond.

Among us, there's Dougie Dugger, who hails from Waco, Texas. He is the founding member of the Heart of Texas Snake Handlers. Then there's Michael Herzog, who joined the Heart of Texas shortly after Dougie. Ken Garrett, my trusted partner in many European escapades, with whom I still hold a world record in the sacking contest. Terry Tippett, from Gatesville, Texas, started his snake-handling journey under Smokey Moore, the same man who plucked that ring from the snake pit. All of us now proudly belong to the Heart of Texas Snake Handlers, one of the few remaining clubs of its kind in the Lone Star State.

Snake handlers are indeed a fickle group, a unique bunch, and being part of such a subculture often feels like being caught in a soap opera, complete with all the drama. For years, I chose to be a lone wolf. I came to all the snake shows and interacted with everybody in all the clubs, and I was primarily involved in the sacking contest because that was one of the things that I was so good at.

It was a skill that earned me an impressive collection of over a hundred trophies. My journey into club life began reluctantly with the Texas Rattlers, and the primary reason why I joined the club was mainly because of a crush I had on one of its members, Betty, who later became my wife in a memorable ceremony surrounded by slithering snakes. Truth be told, I wasn't keen on being part of a club. I kind of wanted to be independent because I knew if I was in that club, I was going to have to be subjected to some rules. Actually, there are a lot of unwritten rules in the subculture of snake handling. And the most important one is respect for other snake handlers. Just like any business in the world, we, too, find ourselves running into some difficulty there every now and again. Some of the handlers may have a little bit of trouble giving the other handlers the respect that they deserve. We recognize most of us as egomaniacs.

But that is quite normal in this business because we probably wouldn't be doing what we do if we didn't have some egotistical issue. But we do have to be really careful when some other handler wants to do something.

We let each handler do what they feel comfortable doing, and they take their own risk. And we help them. We'll do anything they ask us to do within reason. But it's always at their own peril.

Back in the day, when I first dipped my toes into the world of snake handling in 1969, there were a lot of clubs dotting the landscape.

There were names like the Venomairs, Fang Finders, Texas Rattlers, Heart of Texas, and Diamondback Hunters, which were very well-known among snake handlers. Those were just some of the clubs that were around many, many years ago.

Rattlesnake Roundups were a common occurrence, so much so that sometimes clubs had to split up to cover multiple events in different towns simultaneously. At its peak, Texas had around 40 Rattlesnake Roundups each spring and fast forward to today, and the competition has shifted considerably.

The heyday of rattlesnake wrangling has passed, and now, there are about two, maybe three clubs in Texas. Among them is the Heart of Texas, of which I proudly serve as vice president, with Dougie Duggar as president. Another notable club is the Cowboys from Hell.

Now, all these guys are guys that have been in the Heart of Texas club before, and they're good snake handlers and just as I mentioned earlier about giving people respect, I respect these guys to the utmost. I've worked with all of them before, but I'm not a big fan of the name of their group because I'm a Christian man. I don't always show, and I know it probably doesn't look like it sometimes, but I am. So, I have an issue with them calling themselves the Cowboys from hell, But that's up to them, not me.

I don't handle their shows. I said I'd go to some of their shows sometimes, But I usually kind of stay out of their way, and I don't bother them, and they certainly don't bother us or come to our shows anymore. Over the years, I've had the privilege of working alongside them, including Landon

Schultz, David Eastup, and Dave Thomas, and I always offer them my utmost admiration and support.

Working in the world of snake handling requires a deep understanding of the unwritten rules and a heightened sense of awareness. While each club may have its own set of bylaws and regulations, there's a broader code of conduct that goes beyond the individual affiliations.

When we gather at roundups and are surrounded by spectators and sometimes influenced by alcohol, it's crucial to tread carefully. After all, we're dealing with potentially dangerous situations that demand our utmost caution. The achievements I've accomplished, from world records to television appearances and international travels, would have been impossible without the support of individuals like Dougie Duggar, Ken Garrett, Terry Tippett, and Mike Herzog. And, of course, now my son Michael Bibby. Been handling it for fifteen years without a bite.

These men are more than just friends; they're like family to me. We've stood together through thick and thin, helping each other reach our shared goals and dreams.

But it's more than that; I suppose it is about how well we understand each other in an unspeakable manner.

We all have, at some point in our lives, dodged the bullet of death, and The Grim Reaper has greeted us all. Dougie had stage four cancer and recovered. He was on a feeding tube for a while. We did a big benefit for him.

He was at death's door, but God wasn't through with him yet, so he came back, and he's doing good. Michael had a heart attack and had to be given Remote Medevac. He had some people working on him. His heart was stopped for thirty or forty minutes, but luckily, he had some really good first responders, and they kept that heart with the blood flowing while he was on that helicopter until they could get him to a hospital in Waco.

He was in another little town, Clifton, and he had people working on him that kept him alive, and by God's amazing grace, he came out of that with no serious brain damage. I mean, he's got a little bit of a problem remembering some things, but I mean, here's this guy that should have, for all purposes, been dead. If we hadn't had those first responders doing what they did, he would have been.

Terry Tippet has had breast cancer. That's rare in men, of course, but he had to have one of his breasts removed from the cancer. He's come back from that. I, myself, had a blood clot in my lung. Had to be careful.

I was in the hospital for a month. Of course, I was in the hospital over my leg getting off. So, all of us, five core members of the Heart of Texas Snake Handlers, we've stood by each other at death's door. We are battlefield-tested men, and when you've got somebody you've made friends with in a foxhole, they're friends for life.

These guys are just like family to me. They're friends for life. And, you know, when we're setting up late at night in a motel room somewhere during one of these shows, we talk about everything. We know pretty much everything about each other. It's been an amazing journey, and I'm glad mine's not quite over yet.

# Chapter Four

## Jails and Institutions

Jail is a prison for humans gone wrong, someone not behaving. It is a necessity, but for some, prisons are nothing but a time-out like a toddler who is, as punishment, told to face the wall and think about what they did, just like putting people behind bars; perhaps some time alone would clear the head. But then again, sometimes you just need some time alone to think of things.

We are so wild, scared, and crazy that we never have that alone time. We are scared to be alone, but loneliness is just an inescapable feeling. One way or another, it gets you. Those who embrace it live, and those who don't are cursed from running away from it forever.

Personally, I felt the same about jail. I hated it, the idea of it, the smell of it, the confinement of it. And for what? So I could have a moment to think about myself. I'd pass. As if my life wasn't miserable enough, if anything, everything I had ever done that put me in there was to forget myself and enjoy. Either way, we were connected; it was like my home calling to me I would do anything to get in there, but cursing it through when I was in there.

Honestly, I haven't been there because some cop thought he could do anything to me, nor was I black. I just deserved it. For someone who loathed the idea of jail, I sure did manage to get there a lot. As I said, it's for the better when you're in jail, especially if you are fond enough to visit it again; even loved ones find it best for all.

But at the same time, there he was, my father, who did not like me in jail. Of course, no father does, but after some time, they just grow to it, but not him. He made it pretty hard for me to go to jail, and he always saw to it that I didn't stay there long when I did it.

He taught it all to me, so this ugly part was also just another part of him. He did so. I did it too like it was my responsibility, a way to tell him and prove that I was his son. That in my veins, among the venom, ran his blood too. Not that he was to blame for it, he did what he thought was right.

This one time, running away from what I don't seem to recall, I went to the bar and got drunk. Alone, I roamed the streets of my little town. Barely I could walk, but I did so, no mirror to show me how funny I looked, how pitiful, thank God for that. I was having fun. For the fun, I was terrorizing my town, bothering people, making fun of them, shoving them, asking them for a fight. I just wanted to fight someone, anyone. To punch and then take some. Soon, people joined the show in the parking lot of a local truck group; they gathered around to watch me stumble my steps, laughing but mumbling, my arms up with a crazy smile and eyes barely open. "Come on," I said. I had no cause, no motive. This was all me just living. Before I could make any more fool out of sorry myself, a local cop came over. He knew I was drunk. Matter of fact, I was sure we had met before like it was déjà vu but a misery to it. He pulled me aside and asked me to cool my jets. So, I did, not that I was angry. He didn't arrest me. No handcuffs, no lecture, no nothing, just him asking me to come down and meet him down at the city hall, and so I did.

It was about three or four blocks away from the parking lot. Without complaining, I got there as I was told to do. It was night, but not that late, around eight or nine on the clock. Once there, I was greeted by the mayor of our little town.

So now, my audience was skimmed down to that cop and the mayor and a little book they had. With a big sigh, they opened the book and started coming up with charges, and in no time, I guess they came up with five charges I didn't bother to even look upon.

I was drunk; I probably would have caused it. Either way, I was expecting a few words of advice or maybe some curses, but this one had intended to put me behind bars for a time. I did not like it one bit. In fact, it scared me.

"Can I have my phone call, please?" I asked them, drunk and mumbling.

This meant that I had no way out, and I screwed up a little. They allowed it, so I called him, and over the phone, I briefed him and asked him to come down here. Our house was about three or four blocks from city hall, and knowing what was up, he was there in just a few minutes.

Now, the mayor and the cop began explaining how I was terrorizing the people of this town at the truck shop. Patiently, my father, calm and composed, read all the charges.

He handed them back, and after a long pause and silence, he finally said, *"He is going home with me. Now."* He made it pretty clear with his tone that he did not come for a negotiation. The cop tried, and the mayor tried some more, but their efforts were in vain as, to him, it was about pride.

Leaving behind a child is what the worst of the worst do, and my old man had his principles.

"If y'all have any charges, press it. He's coming with me, and we'll see you in court tomorrow if y'all desperate."

That's it. That's what he said, and just like that we were out, and I never heard anything from the cops after that day.

It wasn't any big of a deal back then. But this is now; those things I did get away with. I know I could never get away with what my dad did back then in any town today. But back in the 50s and 60s, 70s, nobody in this town crossed my dad. And when it came to me and my sister, you mess with us, you mess with him. And he'd make your life miserable. I went home and slept like there was no tomorrow.

Back in those days, as an underage kid, if you were caught drinking alcohol, you would get charged with minor-in-possession. It was a big deal, an insult to your parents, and an embarrassment for you.

Anyone who ever received that charge, which was the rarest occurrence in town, would be hailed as a badass by young kids, but you'd be a shameful eyesore for adults. I, for one, had about twenty-one to forty minor possessions before I even turned twenty-one. I was different.

But I turned things around. The last minor-in-possession I ever received was just days before I turned twenty-one. Once I was that age, the world was in the palm of my hand.

I had energy, ambition, anger, and the adrenalin. I was off the hook, slightly inclining towards crazy. That age meant freedom to me. I could do anything, and I'd be held responsible for it. The world was no longer going to treat me like I was some kid. But my will to do something was unsupervised.

I had all these moods, adventure, and craziness, yet I knew what to do with it. The music roared, and the curses grew louder, but I knew what I was going to do. I had the stage, authority, and power. I just needed to claim it. Just as I paid goodbyes to my favorite therapeutic activity, I was ready to step into a newer world, a better one.

Nothing ever comes to an end. Death is not the end, nor is time. Things just change. They are replaced with a wilder, bolder, reckless version. A new start. I was introduced to DWI just before my 21st birthday.

I was drunk and driving, I was caught, and I was arrested, and I thank the god I was. But this one was special. This was the first time ever I would spend a night in jail. Hence would start a series of visits, a place of my calling. The place I hated but deserved to be in.

However, my first time was short-lived. The very next day, I was bailed out by my daddy.

Truth be told, it was no biggie for me. I expected to be scared, but I wasn't. It was just a misdemeanor because it was my first DWI. And I took advantage of the moment too, as at the time, I wasn't quite twenty-one years old, just about to be. Probably turned the age by the time the case went to court. Daddy paid a little fine and I only ended up getting just a six-month probation.

I had signs of trouble addictions to alcohol before I even turned twenty-one. But in all seriousness, I didn't really care; it was all normal to me, and besides, what does a twenty-something kid know about the addictive disorder? How would I cope with it? I had no chance against so I just gave in, straight to the dungeon, a pit that absorbed me and drained me of life.

Call it fate, but I was in it, stuck, lost, and clueless. But it was love. I fell in love with the taste of it, the warmth of it, the subtlety of it, how it lured me, drained me, emptied my mind. I just fell for it. Love took me places, and soon, I was in a place where loving alcohol wasn't enough.

The void in me just grew bigger and bigger, and oceans of alcohol weren't enough. I needed something strong, something that would make me feel things. I ignored it, the voices that called out the names of the drugs, my heart that would lure me whenever I was near them, but I knew very well I was going to try them.

I was the first one in my high school to have access to drugs. One of my friends had an older sister who graduated from my school. She was going with a motorcycle guy who rode with a club called The Chosen Few out of Dallas, Texas. We bumped a little, and with some acquaintance, we, in no time, became good friends.

Or, if I phrase it differently, my attention-seeking desires asked me to be a thug, so he took me under his wings. But the two of us hit it off quite well and given him being only a few years older than I made it easier for me. And in the casualty, he started hooking me up with marijuana in the Rising Star.

This is back in the '60s, and in small towns like Rising Star, Texas, marijuana was rare. You didn't see it much. This guy knew people too well; he'd bring me a matchbox full of manicured marijuana. Once you get the taste of it, you become the master of it. In no time, so I could roll five joints out of it. Well, after this, the path is set for you, it becomes quite predictable, and in that, I started selling joints for a dollar a piece.

I could clear two joints for two dollars because I'd pay three bucks for a matchbox full of marijuana. Selling marijuana was cool, but something even cooler would be when I walked down the halls of my high school, I would hear the whispers of kids saying Jackie Bibby sells drugs. I'd hear that from time to time. I became a go-to guy. I got the attention, and it made my horses run. I craved it, loved it, cherished it.

My first felony was for selling pot. Let's just say some guy asked me to hook him with some marijuana, and like a good business, I delivered. However, his payment was getting me into trouble. Given that this town didn't have much marijuana in just a few months, there was an alarming rise in the consumption, so the forces got to work, and as the tale goes, it was an undercover guy.

But that's all business; it happens to everyone, so that wasn't a big deal. The problem was that my dad was the one that had to arrest me. Now, my dad was the constable of our area. He was elected for nine years. He was in law enforcement for the majority of his life, although at the side, he did some other jobs as well. He had to arrest me and take me in for that charge of selling marijuana to a Narc.

Of course, he took me in over there, checked me into jail, and then paid my bail and bonded me back out. But it was really awkward. I went back home with him, and good for me that he knew a high-dollar lawyer out of Abilene.

However, the lawyer told me, "I'll get you out this time. I'll get you probation, but don't come back to see me if you get in trouble again."

In the end, I was given five years' probation, and I don't know how, but I somehow lived it down because I didn't change anything.

It was in college when I found out what later would become my drug of choice, and it was horrific.

Speed, Methamphetamine, Amphetamine, Hydrochloride, Amphetamine sulfate—it didn't matter. I was just addicted. And I liked it a lot. It came to a point where I started eating pills. Soon, I started snorting it and then started shooting it. When I was on the fresh high on speed, I was a cool daddy supreme. Rich girl's playboy and a poor girl's dream. But boy, did it take a toll on the quality of my life.

When I got busted the second time, the price of poker went way up. I got caught selling two and a half ounces of meth to a DPS narcotic segment. The DA's first offer was twenty-five years, and I was screwed badly this time. And once again, it was my dad, coming to save my ass for my reckless, spent, empty, hollow life. He was my father, and he did what any father would do. He started pulling strings, calling in favors, and developing a plan.

Thanks to a really sharp psychiatrist named Dr. Theodore Tarasevich, a Russian man. I made several trips to the nut house because I kept having to go to where that doctor worked at San Antonio State Hospital. In the end, the old man had to pay $68,000 to get me a probation instead of going to the penitentiary.

It was kind of funny because that DA was terrified of that psychiatrist. That psychiatrist pretty much told him, you'll give him probation, or I'll give him off.

So, they gave me probation. I lived down nine months of that probation before I got busted again. Letting down people who had no hopes for me. That's the worst kind of pain. A man can take the pain of parting, heartbreak from a lover, death in the family, but this. This was a tyrannical pain I caused myself. I was hurting myself, but I didn't care. I was hurting my parents and my sister, and I didn't care. I was heartless. And I deserved pain. But only me, not others.

I had a partner back then. We had this infallible deal that we were running. We drove a cold car that wasn't registered to either of us. I was definitely the one that was under scrutiny at all times. He had never been charged with anything and wasn't very well known.

So, I'd go make the deals and a different car and he'd come along behind me in the cold car. He'd pick up the drugs, take them wherever we needed to take them, sell them. And, of course, he was kind of flunky, but I paid him pretty well for doing it.

One day, he gave out on me. He said, man, I got to sleep.

I said, no, don't sleep, man. Do another shot of dope. We got dope to sell because I can't do it by myself.

But he didn't listen and went to sleep lying on the floor. At that moment, I thought to myself, hell, I can't just sit around here. So, I took an old cap and pulled it down over my eyes. I got in that cold car, and I went selling drugs. But little did I know that that day, there was a snitch.

One of the places where I went sold drugs; he called the Sheriff's Department and informed them what I was driving and what I was wearing, and they got me that day.

I had about an ounce of meth, half an ounce of cocaine, twenty amphetamine pills, black mollies, forty valiums, scales, vials, baggies, and a pistol. All in a little flight bag in the trunk of my car, wrapped up nice and neat, my death sentence. They took me to jail, and I filmed a deal about me going to jail and how pictures from back when all that went down.

I was thirty-five, and one of the trustees there at the jail named Billy Brown. He sat me down, and he told me this: When I heard they were bringing you in, I was so excited I thought, I'm fixing to get to see the biggest drug dealer in Brown County. They brought you in, and I thought, wow. That old man, the drug dealer?

I was thirty-five, and that man thought I was on my last legs. But I couldn't blame him. It was no exaggeration from him. After all, I'm strung out on dope. A thirty-five-year-old looking like a sixty-year-old. The hardest part of it was when my old man came to see me a few days later in a jail cell. It was sad. I wanted to cry, but I ran myself dry. I had nothing left in me.

*'Son, I can't get you out of this.'*

His eyes, I couldn't tell what they meant. Was he sad? That this was what became of his only son. Or was he sad that he couldn't help his only son? Was he mad that his son betrayed him time after time, or was he mad that he couldn't stop his son? I broke him. I broke my old man.

I was cruel to him, to my mother, to my sister. I wondered if this was what I wanted. I wanted to be a star. A star that shines and glimmers in the dark night sky. Here I was, the dark itself. I was rotting, looking nothing like myself, within four walls.

I was given two eight-year sentences running concurrently. One was for probation revocation, and the other one was for the new possession of all that stuff I had in the trunk of my car.

Now, the cell block that I was in when I was out to county jail for the sentiment of prison didn't have bars. It had little squares. There were about three-inch squares. And there was flat metal in between each square. There was no visitation there at their county jail and it served me right. Still, my parents would come twice a week, and they'd let them come up to the tank and visit with me through the cell.

I remember sitting in there, and from between those squares, I would slip my cold fingers. And my mother would hold my fingers with her warm, comforting hands.

It was warm and peaceful. I would feel it, my happiness, which I didn't deserve.

*'Son, you got to pray.'*

*'I can't.'* I'd tell her.

*'Well, I'll pray for you till you can.'*

She did. I needed them. I wanted them. I desperately did. But I just couldn't myself. My faith had gone senile, dead. But not hers, and it worked. I wish I could say it worked real quick, but it didn't. It was years later. But I was grateful the seed was planted, and God was definitely working in my life.

I did go to prison. It's been a great deal of time down there. Twenty-six months. I met a couple of friends there. Terry Nunn was one of the premier dope cooks in Texas. Johnny Haier was a wet-backed German who went to jail for holding up Safeway stores.

He was a drug addict, too, and was holding those stores up. People with gunpoint work could get drugs. And those two guys kind of took care of me. They were very tough guys, and I wasn't all that tough. I was kind of a hoodlum, but it wasn't tough about me. I could definitely fight if I had to. I could hold my own, but I was kind of skittish on nervous around things.

These guys would laugh about it. They thought it was pretty hilarious, which I guess was because people would go to steal, and the steward department would work.

And I wouldn't steal. I kept telling them, "Guys, I don't steal."

"You're in the penitentiary. Why do you mean you don't steal?"

"I don't steal." I'd tell them.

So, I never did.

I never stole a single thing while I was in the penitentiary, but these guys didn't hold back. They stole a lot of things from me, and that didn't bother them much. When I went to prison, I was kind of a small-town drug dealer. But prison is a finishing school for criminals. When I came out, I had way better connections.

Terry Nunn was one of my closest friends. He's dead now. But we came out of that thing, and we were really tight. He was a really good dope cook, and I was really good at selling it. So, going to prison certainly didn't interrupt my addictive process in any way, unfortunately. If anything, It just made me a lot better at what I was doing.

But during my time from getting out of prison in 1981 to until my time getting recovered in the mid-80s, I went to jail one time. And that was when my dad put me in there. He was so disgusted with my behavior and all the things I'd torn up and cost.

A company that belonged to our family back then was making really good money. My dad spent it like a drunken sailor, and at me, he was really disgusted. I was kind of pissed with him, and I had problems of my own, so I wrecked about two or three pickups in a car and tore up a bunch of stuff that belonged to the family.

That pissed him off, so he threw two $100 bills at me out on the street in front of our manufacturing plant and said, '*I never want to see you again.*'

That was it for me. It was the beginning of my recovery because my dad had never said no to me. But he was so pissed at me that he arrested me and took me to jail.

We got to the jail, and he started trying to get me locked up and the jailer there thought it was a joke because my dad and

I ran the jail ministry. We used to come over here periodically, take bibles, and hand them out to the inmates.

These Bibles weren't just for spiritual guidance; they also served as a practical item for those headed to prison to keep their papers in. So, as Christians, we were committed to this ministry. But that jailer thought it was a joke, and he would not lock me up, which made him even more furious. He was on the verge of blowing a fuse. We went next door across the street to the courthouse over there and went to the DA's office. My dad was ranting and raving to the DA.

"When I bring somebody into jail and tell them to lock them up, I mean lock them up. I don't care who he is."

He was serious and had no intention of going back without having me locked up. There was an attorney sitting there in the DA's office. I didn't recognize him. Didn't know who he was. I was a little paranoid.

So, I decided maybe I needed to give him a whipping. I grabbed him by the lapels and pushed him up against the wall. That got me in jail. They arrested me, put me in handcuffs, and escorted me to the jail, where I was locked up for eight days. They were committing me to a treatment center. That was the first time I'd ever gone to any institution for drug addiction. I've been many times for the things that were wrong in my head, and believe me, I was certifiably insane. But nobody could do drugs and drink and live the way I did and not be insane.

So, they didn't have any trouble qualifying me to go to state hospitals or private mental institutions.

Since being in prison and since the mid-1980s, after I got into recovery, I've been to jail one other time. That was for whipping my son. He was fifteen years old. He got expelled from school two times in the same week. The second time when I picked him up from school, on the way home, I roughed him up a little bit and this soft boy wasn't all that. He wasn't used to that. This poor boy wasn't used to me ever getting very angry, very upset.

So when we got home, this rascal jumped out of the car and went to the house and called the police and told him that I was beating him. The next thing I knew, I was in jail, arrested for domestic violence.

Sometime during the next day, my dad came over and my wife at the time, Karen, helped, and they got me out of jail. With a good lawyer and a lot of money, I got those charges dropped. But obviously, after I got into recovery, I finally learned how to live without getting in trouble with the law very often.

I guess I am the only person whose father and son had him arrested on two different occasions. But I guess it was these bitter pills that helped me change my life.

I know I let my parents down with my drug addiction, but it struck me a lot now about them coming to save time after time again, and I suppose that's because they understood. They've been through all this. We are unlucky in terms of our drug abuse as a family, but that's what makes us understand one another so well.

# Chapter Five

## Feel Good, Act Bad

It was early in my life when I first suffered from ingesting a substance. It was certainly not in my best interest. I was only three days old. I got very sick and almost died—*almost*.

It turned out that my mom's milk was too rich for me, and it was messing up my digestive tract. Thankfully, the doctor figured it out, and they got me on formula.

Of course, I believe God just had big plans for me, which I can see now.

Moving on, my first drug of choice—my first poison, was beer.

I don't even remember my first taste of beer. But what I remember is the second I tasted it, I liked it. My dad, along with both my grandfathers, gave me sips of their beer.

For as long as I can remember, when I was a kid, my parents went to country dances. All of us kids got really good at sneaking open beers while the grownups were dancing. We'd form a circle, pass it around until it was gone, and then sneak back in to steal another one.

All addicts have a predisposition for addiction, no matter the substance or the behavior. For example, alcohol.

My predisposition was very strong. My mom was an addict, my dad was an addict, and my grandfather on my dad's side, Papa Jack, was a raging alcoholic. He died at eighty-four, and toward the end of his life, he liked to say he had quit drinking, but he still bought Listerine by the case.

My drunkenness and drug abuse could fill a book in and of itself, but in an effort to qualify myself as a member of several 12-step fellowships, I'll tell a few stories, starting with alcohol, my first drug of choice.

Although I previously stated I do not recall my first drink of alcohol, I do remember the first time my dad gave me my own beer to drink. It was my senior year.

We were in Okra, Texas, headed for Eastland.

Dad said, "Give me a beer."

As I handed him one, he said, "You can have one too."

And oh, that was a good beer!

I remember it like it was yesterday. An obvious indication I was a fledgling alcoholic.

Fast-forward to 1968, when I graduated high school. Just a couple of days before our graduation, we had a baccalaureate service. My dear friend Carl Clark and I got to celebrate before the service, so when we got there, we were drunk.

I made it through the processional pretty well, but when we had to stand for prayer and I closed my eyes, I realized it was a terrible idea.

Thankfully, my good friend Debbie Medley was right beside me. She steadied me, saved me from falling, and helped me get through the rest of the service. Still, it was very obvious that Carl and I were plastered.

As a result, we got expelled from school for two of the last three days of our high school year and were forced to take all our finals in one day. But because God loves drunks and idiots, we did get to graduate.

In 1969, I attended CJC. My friend Carl rode with me. One day, we went to Ranger, picked up a six-pack, and headed back to class.

On the way, I picked up a hitchhiker, a young boy from Florida, headed to California to join a commune called the Gold Diggers.

I got the bright idea to leave Carl with my car and let him take it back to my dad and hit the road with the hitchhiker.

And so, we set off. On our way out to West Texas, we stopped in Midland and ate pastries from a day-old bakery.

Sitting by a railroad track, the boy remarked, "It ain't all that good, but it sure is filling."

Not long after, we made it to El Paso. There, I lost my nerve. I told him he could go on ahead and I was going to stay. I spent the first night on an old bus behind a filling station. A guy working at the station let me inside the bus, locked it behind me, and promised to get me out before he left for work.

Early the next morning, I woke up scared to death, thinking he'd forgotten me. I squeezed through one of the bus windows, scraping myself in the process, and fell out on my head, only to discover that he hadn't left work yet and was about to come get me out.

I roamed around town that day and spent the second night in the foyer of a bowling alley. The next day, I called my dad and asked if I could come home.

He said, "I never asked you to leave."

Anyway, my dad called a cousin of his whom I had never met. They came and got me, took me to their house, fed me a meal, let me take a shower, and put me to bed. The next day, they put me on a bus and sent me back home.

I was doing so poorly in school at the time that it was suggested I drop out and restart. Over the next semester, it was advised that I try to get a withdrawal passing (WP) from all my classes, not a withdrawal failing (WF) because a WF didn't look as good on the transcript.

So, I concocted a story that my dad had been working in the oil field, had a horrible accident, and got his leg cut off—*a bit of irony there.*

I claimed that due to that accident, I hadn't been in school recently, which explained my poor performance, and that I wanted to withdraw so I could start fresh next semester. Four out of five professors bought my story and gave me a WP. One did not, and I got a WF in that class.

I went back and completed three semesters, somehow managing to earn twenty-four or twenty-five hours of credit.

*I was putting most of my effort into drinking and chasing girls.*

My college deferment was in danger. It was the early seventies, the Vietnam War was ongoing, and I had a terrible number in the draft lottery. I wasn't keen on the idea of going to Vietnam.

Once again, my dad stepped in. One of his big ideas was to get me into the National Guard. So, we started looking around, and on short notice, there was only one Guard unit accepting people—*a National Guard Airborne Unit in Stephenville, Texas.*

I thought, *'Well, I wouldn't mind jumping out of airplanes.'*

So, we got involved, and I joined the National Guard.

Three days after receiving my draft notice, my dad lied to the draft board, telling them I hadn't been home in weeks and had already been sworn into the National Guard. I never knew I had received a draft notice. Somehow, we pushed that through and got away with it.

I had just under six months of active duty. I went to basic training and received an accommodation for scoring over 475 out of 500 on a physical training test.

I qualified as an expert on every weapon they let me shoot. Then, I went to AIT for infantry and then to jump school.

Jump school was three weeks long. The first week, they separated the men from the boys. In the second week, they separated the boys from the idiots. And the third week, we idiots jumped. I stayed for three years and eleven months.

At that time, our family had a thriving business, a sewing factory. In 1976, we won the Governor's Small Business Award. We had fifty-one employees. My dad was working three jobs, which was pretty much normal for him, and he suffered two heart attacks.

Due to my father's heart attacks, we decided it would be an excellent opportunity for me to finish out my military duty. So, we filed the paperwork and got a hardship discharge for me to run the company business because of my dad's health issues.

But let me tell you how my dad handled those heart attacks. After the second one, the doctor told him very clearly not to go back to work and that he needed to rest. My mom picked him up from the hospital, and as they were approaching the red light near our house, Dad said, "Take me by the shop."

She protested, reminding him of the doctor's orders, but he insisted, "I said, take me by the shop."

So, she drove him there, and he went back to work. He never missed another day after that. To the best of my knowledge, my dad had a very clear philosophy and my sister, my mom, and I knew it well. We did what he said without question, and he did whatever he wanted to do, also without question. It never served us well to challenge him.

My dad was a very double-standard, confusing man. Now, I believe he was an untreated addict, though he never admitted it. I think his denial was genuine.

He could be mean, cruel, hateful, and violent, but by the same token, he could be kind, gentle, and loving. He was well thought of and respected in our community. He did many good things for many people and spoiled my mom, my sister, and me.

But he'd still whip any or all of us and then love on us and tell us he was sorry.

My first drug of choice was bad and caused me a lot of misery and chaos, but my next drug of choice—stimulants like speed, meth, coke, and amphetamines—was a hundred times worse.

Oh, not at first.

When I first started getting high on stimulants, I thought, *'I have arrived. This is the answer to all my problems.'*

Over the course of eighteen years, I made the journey that every garden-variety addict makes: a downward dip to the bottom, followed by a vicious spiral. I changed wives and girlfriends, and I ended up in mental institutions.

I went to jail. I went to prison. I did everything negative you could do except die. Thank goodness for a gracious and merciful God who was looking after me. He had big plans for me.

While I was in prison from 1979 through 1981, I met a man who became a lifelong friend. His name was Terry Nunn. He had a seventh-grade education, and was one of the smartest men I ever knew. But it was street smarts, not book learning.

Terry was a real outlaw, and I was a wannabe. He took me under his wing and looked out for me until the day he died.

Terry had a knack for running off with my wives and girlfriends, but he always brought them back.

One time, he even ended up in prison for shooting at me. He had run off with my third wife, Betty Lou, and after a couple of days, he brought her back. But he kept coming to the door, wanting to talk to her. I finally ran him off with a straight razor.

That same day I had some dope spread out on a piece of glass on the headboard of my bed. I was picking out the rocks for my private stash. Betty was watching when a shot rang out. A bullet came through the window, missing my head by about six inches and hitting the wall right next to me.

I ducked, hit the glass, and knocked an ounce of dope all over the room into the shag carpet. We picked the dope out of that carpet for days.

But back to the story, the bullet missed me and Betty called the sheriff's office and told them Terry was shooting at us. They caught him with the gun still in his car, and he went back to jail and then to prison.

The next day, I went to the county jail and put money on his books. I wasn't all that mad at him. If he had wanted to shoot me, he would have. He was just trying to scare me, and it worked.

After Terry got out of prison, he went back to cooking dope, and it wasn't long before I started selling it for him. It was very lucrative. Once we got the lab set up, we could buy the chemicals for about $700 or $800, and that would make about twenty pounds.

We were fronting it out for $10,000 a pound. If we got between $5,000 and $10,000 back, we'd front him another pound. We were making a lot of money, but we were as crazy as a tree full of hoot owls, and none of that money seemed to stick.

I'm pleased and proud to report that Terry eventually got a good wife, settled down, and stayed clean and law-abiding for the last few years of his life. It was a huge blessing to me that I got to spend about two hours with him just a few days before he passed.

Later, when we got clean, Terry and I would attend church together. He and his wife, Rhonda, would come to the

Cowboy Church with me, and I would go to the Biker Church with them.

One time, when I was visiting the Biker Church, I told the pastor before the service that Terry and I used to sing in the choir when we were in prison together and that our favorite song was *Victory in Jesus*.

During his message, the pastor called me and Terry up and told the congregation the story about us singing in the prison choir and how much we loved *Victory in Jesus*. He then asked us to lead the congregation in the song.

We led a rousing rendition of Victory in Jesus, but Terry was so embarrassed he could've killed me, because he didn't crave attention like I did.

If I detail my entire drug saga, this chapter would be longer than the rest of the entire book. So, let me conclude by sharing what became the beginning of the end of my *using* career.

I was hanging around Waxahachie, Texas, driving my dad's old pickup. I was broke and trying to convince my wife to bring her three kids and come back to live with me in Rising Star.

*It wasn't going well.*

I had just gotten out of jail, and a cop I knew suggested that if I set up my wife's boyfriend, he'd let me stay out of trouble. Desperate, I agreed and didn't even care if the boyfriend knew I did it.

I managed to scrape together a little dope and gave some to my wife, telling her to pass it to her boyfriend as a peace offering. I convinced her that if we could just see a marriage counselor, we could work things out. I just needed to get that boyfriend locked up, thinking she might then be willing to bring the kids and come back home.

Later that day, the boyfriend showed up at my wife's house. I met him in the front yard, looked him in the eyes, and said, "I'm supposed to set you up."

He replied, "Yeah, I'm supposed to set you up too."

I ran him off and went inside, where I got into a huge fight with my wife. In the heat of the moment, I forced her into the pickup with me, and we took off. As we drove away, fighting and hitting each other, her son and one of his friends jumped into her TransAm and took off after us.

They pulled alongside me, trying to get me to stop, but I didn't. So, they started shooting at the pickup with a 12-gauge shotgun, hitting it twice. I sped up, and then when they got alongside me again, I stomped on the brakes, letting them pass. Then I sped up and rammed into the back of their car, spinning it out into a ditch and totaling it.

Right after that, I noticed a cop following us. He must have seen everything, but he didn't even stop me.

I didn't understand why. Something was definitely going on. Soon, we encountered several more cops. There were cars on both sides of the road, and cops were standing outside, holding up their arms and hollering for me to stop, but there was no roadblock. So, I kept on going.

I asked Betty, "Is there something going on? Do you know what it is?"

She said, "Yes, I do."

Then turned to me, "The cops gave me some lab chemicals to plant on you. They were going to bust you and put you in prison so I would be safe, but I was more afraid of you than I was of them. So, I threw the chemicals in the creek."

When the cops finally stopped me, it was almost dark. They pulled me out from behind the pickup, cuffed me, and told Betty to drive and get out of there.

She took off, and they hauled me to jail in Bosque County, Meridian, Texas. I spent a couple of days there and had this little scam going that I found amusing.

I told everyone in the jail—other inmates, trustees, and even the cops—that someday I was going to make a movie about this, and they better be nice to me, or I'd let someone ugly play them.

They called my dad and tried to get him to come get me. He told them he didn't want me.

Eventually, they let me out on a personal recognizance bond—*whatever that is*.

I took off on foot from the jail and started hitchhiking toward Waxahachie. Soon, an old man and a young man who said they had been fishing picked me up. They offered me a beer, and I accepted. I started drinking my beer and telling my story about Waxahachie.

We hadn't gone very far when the young man said, "Son, we're federal officers, and we're getting tired of messing with you."

The older guy said, "You can't tell him that."

The young man replied, "Yeah, this SOB needs to know. If he goes back to Waxahachie, he might end up getting shot."

I asked them to stop, and I got out and started hitchhiking in the other direction. When I finally got back to Rising Star, my dad was not happy. My wife had called and told him where the pickup was left.

He and I went to retrieve it, and when he saw the gunshots in the side and the smashed front end, his mood didn't improve much.

By the time we got back to Rising Star, my dad threw two $100 bills at me and said, "I never want to see you again."

I roughed him up pretty good. He arrested me and took me to jail. You've already heard the story about the jailer not locking me up because he thought it was a joke. But I did manage to get myself locked up, and I was in jail for eight days before being brought to court and committed to the State Hospital Substance Program in Wichita Falls, Texas.

# Chapter Six

## Recovery Works If You Work It

It was the summer of 1986. Here I was, back in jail. For the first two or three days, I thought I was there for roughing up my dad. Then, I got word that I was being committed to the SARP unit at Wichita Falls Treatment Center for addiction. When I arrived at the SARP unit, it was intriguing. I had never been to a place that addressed addicts as a primary focus, that treated addiction as a primary dysfunction. These people knew me better than I knew myself. I fell right into the routine, and in no time, I thought I had the counselors dancing in the palm of my hand. I was sure I had charmed all the girls in treatment with me.

During my second week there, they let me have a visit. My parents came to see me. I had asked my mom to bring me a sack of stuff that was on my dresser. She had no idea what it was, and even if she had looked into it, she still wouldn't have known. The sack had butyl nitrate in it. Butyl nitrate is not illegal, but it is used to get high. To give you an idea of how sick I was, I thought that since it wasn't illegal, it was okay. I was shocked when, on Monday morning, they called me into a meeting and asked if I had butyl nitrate on the unit.

"Yes," I answered and pulled it out of my pocket, placing it on the table.

As it turned out, I got myself, and six others who admitted to using with me kicked out of treatment. If everyone who used with me had been caught, they would have had to close down the unit. I was shocked and, in my sick mind, thought they were mistreating me horribly. So, I took off from the state hospital on foot with my suitcase and started hitchhiking toward Waxahachie.

Halfway to Dallas, I got picked up by a guy in a gravel truck. His name was Billy Bob. I told him about getting kicked out of the SARP unit.

"I've been to that program before," he said.

We buddied up pretty well. I asked him if I bought some beer, would he like to drink it with me. He agreed, and I bought us a six-pack. We tore that up pretty quickly, and he had to make a turn, so he let me out. I kept on going toward Waxahachie, but Billy Bob would turn up again.

I was on my way to Waxahachie, where my wife was, and thought about a close friend from school, Grant Poyner. We started first grade together and graduated twelve years later.

We were close friends and stayed at each other's houses frequently. Grant went to the Marine Corps, and after he got out, he became an attorney. We stayed in contact; we were lifelong friends. We still are.

I called him and told him my story of what was going on.

"As soon as I get off work, I'll come get you," he said.

He did and took me to his apartment in North Dallas. I stayed with him for several days. My obsessive focus was on how everybody was mistreating me: my wife, the cops, and the treatment center. My friend Grant was a member of AA, which I did not know. I'm pretty sure it was God doing for me what I was unwilling to do for myself. While I was complaining, my friend was talking program to me, which was not soaking in much at all.

One day, while my friend was at work, I was watching the 700 Club on TV. A man came on the program and said he was a drug addict and that there was someone out there who was also an addict. He started praying, and so did I. I don't remember much of what he said, but I remember I was crying and feeling a little bit better. I got on my knees, held onto a desk in my friend's room, and listened to that program.

The next day, I rode a bus downtown to an NA meeting. I know I'd been to meetings before, but this is the first one I actually remember. So, I started attending every day. I'm country, so being in the city kind of scared me. Within the first couple of days, Grant gave me the money to buy an NA book.

When I started reading it, I was amazed that it was a book about me. When I got my first NA book, I read most of it that first night. The next day, when I went to the meeting, I remembered the book said to ask to help. So, after the meeting, I went to the chairperson and asked if there was anything I could do to help.

"Bring me those brochures," he said.

I went over to the rack, pulled them out, stacked them up all nice and neat, and took them to him. He thanked me, and I went away beaming. Just as I was leaving the meeting hall, I saw him putting them back into the rack. He had just given me something to do, but it made me feel a lot better.

My mom and dad knew I had been kicked out of treatment. They did not know where I was. I finally called and told them that I was at Grant's and that I wanted to go back to treatment. Grant put me on a bus, and my dad picked me up. They court committed me again. My dad took me back to the treatment center, and I recall that the counselor who checked me in said they were not pleased to have me back. But since I was court-committed, they had to accept me. They told me they were going to watch me like a hawk. They did, but I completed treatment at that time.

I tried really hard and was excited, thinking I had it figured out. My second time around, my nickname was Buzz Saw.

One of the men in my group told me, "Jackie, you could charm a bird out of a tree. If bull shit was ten cents a ton, you'd be a millionaire."

With the help of a power greater than myself, which I choose to call God, I did complete treatment that time. My parents came to my graduation.

One of my counselors told my dad, "Don't give him any money or anything to drive unless he's going to work, a meeting, or to school."

I thought that was cruel, but actually, it was a very good suggestion.

So, I found myself at my parents' house: no home, no car, no job, and pretty much even with the world. I owed about as many people as I didn't. But I had about a month clean, and that was different. I started attending meetings every day. At this stage in my recovery, I was a bit naive.

I thought, *'I got this. I'll never use again.'*

It was shortly after getting a 90-day chip that I experienced what relapse is all about. I had this girl—it's always a girl with me. We went through treatment together and were talking on the phone. I made plans to come see her. I had big plans for a romantic encounter. Turns out she had already relapsed, and she wanted to know if I had any money to buy her some drugs, implying, of course, that romance would be forthcoming. I bought her some dope—heroin, not even my drug of choice.

But somehow, my dope fiend came out, and I wound up using with her. It made me sick as a dog. No romance, and I drove home sick, depressed, disappointed, and sad. But thank goodness, I went right back to meetings and reestablished early recovery.

I went back to school. I was thirty-five years old, a non-traditional student. It was the first time I'd ever gone to school to learn. The youngsters there hated me. I sat in the front row and asked lots of questions. When I was in treatment, I had asked one of the counselors what it took to be a substance abuse counselor. I guess most of us who ever cleaned up thought we were going to save the world. That counselor gave me the requirements and put them up on the board. It was a pretty long list.

Then, in front of about fifty people, he told me, "Bibby you'll never make a counselor. It's too much work."

I was so angry at him. It was years before I had the aha experience. He had just motivated me. So, in early recovery, I went back to Cisco College for one semester, then transferred to Tarleton State University in pursuit of a social work degree. I lacked six hours to get a bachelor's degree, but I couldn't pass algebra. I took it four times and finally just gave up on school. I already had a really good job. I was making good money working for a treatment center and working on getting my counselor certificate. I was already a certified outreach specialist, so I wasn't all that worried about that degree. I was making real good money, and I was going to counselor school in Dallas, where I went one weekend a month. In a year, I'd have enough training to get my license.

While going to college full-time, working, and going to counselor school, I heard of a job working in a treatment center not far—twenty miles—from where I was going to college. I applied for the job, lied about my clean time, and got the job. I was a tech in the treatment center at Hico Lodge.

They loved me. I was a glorified babysitter, and of course, with my stories and my tales, all the clients just thought I was great.

I was living in Rising Star, Texas, going to college in Stephenville, which was fifty miles away, working at Hico Lodge, which was another twenty miles from the school, and then sixty miles from home. I was going to counselor school in Dallas once a month, which was a hundred and fifty miles away, and I didn't even have a vehicle.

My dad had a pretty new pickup, and I wore it out that year. I kept the roads hot, and I was on a mission. I finally got a car, an old Mercury Cougar. It was ugly, but it ran.

I hadn't worked for Hico Lodge long, only a few months, and I got a big promotion and a raise. I became a marketer for Hico Lodge. I was going to be a headhunter. I was very effective at that job. I remember my boss, Gary Hunt, buying me some new clothes and a briefcase. I sincerely thought I'd never see another poor day.

I had found my job. I loved my job, my school, my counselor training. My life was good. I was one of the miracles. And by God's amazing grace, a helpless and hopeless drug addict had become a productive member of society.

But it was not a good time to be complacent, nor a great time to get involved with a woman who was using. And one of my good friends, who was also in recovery, was hanging out with this cute girl that we knew who was also going to meetings but was still using. Not that uncommon—everyone gets it at their own pace—but if you hang out in a barbershop long enough, you will wind up getting a haircut.

I wound up using with this girl, and my buddy, who was not using, snitched me off to my boss. My boss heard I had used it, so I did the really smart thing: I went and hid out. I stayed gone for about three days, only talking to my sponsor.

My sponsor kept telling me, "You gotta get honest. You gotta tell Rodney Blanks, who was my boss, everything that you've done wrong."

I didn't really like that idea, but my boss was a great man. He was in recovery also. He had forgotten more about staying clean than I'd ever know. After the three days of hiding, I went to see him. I had a page and a half written on a legal pad of things I had done wrong. I started reading my list, and I wasn't halfway through when he stopped me.

"Okay, you relapsed. Do you want to go to treatment? I'll hold your job for you."

I was stunned. I could not believe he wanted to help me and expressed that I was valuable to his team and that I'd have a job when I completed treatment. So, he sent me to a treatment center in Bridgeport, Texas. I was there not for four weeks but for five. It was very intense. That was the fall of 1988, which is my current clean date: October 15th, 1988.

After that third time in treatment, I have maintained abstinence. Now you know how a hopeless and helpless garden-variety addict finally got clean and became a somewhat productive member of society. I am relatively happy.

This chapter of my life marks a pivotal transformation, demonstrating the resilience of the human spirit and the profound impact of support and faith. Through the trials and relapses, the journey was anything but linear.

Yet, it was these very challenges that fortified my resolve and deepened my commitment to recovery. Each setback was a lesson, each triumph a testament to the power of perseverance.

Today, as I reflect on my journey from a hopeless addict to a productive member of society, I am reminded that recovery is not a destination but a continuous path. With support from friends, family, and God, I have learned that recovery truly works if you work it.

# Chapter Seven

# God's Greatest Inventions—*Food and Women*

I have always said that if God invented anything greater than food and women, he kept it for himself. About thirty years ago, after a 12-step meeting, I learned something very valuable that I have not forgotten. Several men and women were talking and flirting with each other when one of the guys made a comment.

"How come all you ladies love Jackie Bibby so much?" He asked.

This brought a small laugh from the group, and one of the ladies responded, "Jackie B likes women. You don't. You just like to use us."

She was right. I do like women. I love them, I lust after them, and I am constantly in awe of them. But I also give them my utmost respect. It is my belief that men and women put their worlds together in dramatically different ways. By communicating, understanding, and accepting this basic fact, we can have harmonious relationships. In my lifetime, I've had more love and affection than anyone deserves.

Let's talk about some of the amazing ladies I have known. First, there's Betty number one, Betty Ann, my first wife. Betty passed away a few years ago. It was the seventies. We were young and partying hard. Betty Ann was my sister's good friend. We hooked up and had fun. Nothing serious. But we thought we had gotten pregnant, so we had a quick marriage. We thought it was the right thing to do.

It was a beautiful ceremony. We went to Carlsbad Caverns on our honeymoon, and two days after we got home, it became clear that we were not pregnant. Still, we were both determined to do the best we could.

Betty was sweet and kind and tried hard. I was a terrible husband. Although I was never malicious, I hurt us both a lot, so the marriage lasted only about two years. I'm happy to write that Betty remarried and was in a good marriage at the time of her passing. We talked many times, and I think I effectively conveyed to her that I was sorry for being such a poor husband.

My second wife was one of the most amazing people I have ever known. I wish she would let me elaborate in detail, but based on her desire to remain anonymous and out of respect for her and her family's privacy, I will say no more.

My third wife was Betty Lou, or as we often referred to her, Betty Number Two. She was a snake handler, a good one, although she did lose an index finger on her left hand from a bite she received when we were sacking snakes together in Taylor, Texas, at the National Rattlesnake Sacking Contest. Betty and I knew each other because we were both involved in rattlesnake roundups. Back then, I was still independent with no club affiliation. As a result of my huge crush on Betty, she talked me into joining the club she was in, the Texas Rattlers. I had been in the club for only a few days when I was selected as president. I served in that capacity for many years. We traveled a lot and did many snake shows.

Our romance grew rapidly, and soon we were together. It was several years before we got married. I'm very sorry to admit that we did drugs together. Betty handled the drugs better than I did. I regret that I hurt Betty and her kids as a result of my active addiction, but I know they all understand it was never malicious. Some of our escapades related to drugs have already been covered in a previous chapter. Today, I can happily report that Betty and I are good friends and even perform together at snake shows now and then. Betty Lou tried as hard as anybody to be my partner, and we managed to pull it off for several years.

Betty got clean before I did, and it was very traumatic toward the end of my active addiction when she wouldn't come back to me. She became numb to my charm and the bullshit, but I think she played a part in my finally getting clean several years later.

My next torrid love affair was with Anya. We were together for about nine months. It was an amazing time. She was beautiful, charismatic, funny, smart, and very challenging. She worked at a convenience store where I bought a lot of beer. I amped up the charm and the bullshit, spending money like a drunken sailor in the store, and it didn't take long before she was running with me. I talked her into moving in with me. She had wrecked a car that belonged to our company, and my dad and I convinced her she needed to work for the family business to pay for the car repairs. Anya and my dad were big buddies. He liked her about as much as I did.

Once, we were at a party at my cousin's house. One of her best friends was there, and I was flirting with her. Anya got a bit annoyed at me. I had bought her three ounces of pot from my cousin Jet, and on the way home, we got into a fuss. I decided to throw her pot out the window, and after I did, she almost bit my thumb off. The next day, we went back and walked around in the ditches and found two of the three ounces. I guess somebody else found the other one. *Lucky them! Or maybe there were some happy raccoons.*

In another of our great adventures, we took off in my *Good Times* van to the county line. It was twenty-four miles to the nearest beer store. We got a case of beer, started back home on the back roads, and had the bright idea to remove our clothes. We were having a great time drinking, driving, drinking, and driving naked. All was going well until we topped a little hill and drove off into a game warden roadblock. They were stopping people from looking for hunters.

A game warden came to my window with a flashlight, shined it in, and said, "Are y'all hunting?"

I said, "No, we're just playing."

He rocked back on his heels and said, "Well, go on playing then."

Our time was filled with these stories. It was a wild and crazy adventure, very memorable. But as with all of my relationships, my challenges became too much, and Anya moved on. I'm happy to report she married a fine man from

Rising Star. They're happy and thriving to this day, and I'm friends with both of them.

I met Christie Michelle, the mother of my two boys, at a Codependence Anonymous meeting. We had been in the same meetings a few times, and of course, I was flirting with her. My first interaction with her outside of the 12-step meeting was at a grocery store. She was having an altercation with a store clerk over $10. I was right behind her in line and followed her out to the parking lot. I witnessed her put her groceries in an old ragtop Pontiac that looked to me like it was on its last leg.

I remember thinking, *'This girl must be really poor. I'm sure she needed that $10 she was arguing about.'*

It was several months later that I came to know she was married to a very wealthy man who restored cars. That old car was one he was restoring at that time, and it was worth way more than my car.

It is often said that opposites attract. That couldn't have been more apparent than with Christie and me. Our only common interest was that we both liked to fly airplanes. Oh yeah, there was one other thing, but you know, there was plenty of attraction. We were friends for a while before we started having an affair. Shortly thereafter, she became pregnant.

In Texas, you can't get a divorce if you're expecting, so we did a paternity test and established paternity. In May of 1991, Michael Edward Bibby was born. Eventually, Christie got a divorce, and we changed Michael's name to Bibby. We lived together for several years and hardly ever had a crossword. We both loved our sons and each other to a degree, but there wasn't much else aside from mutual respect. We were not that great at being romantic partners, but we are still great friends.

When Michael was born, we had to establish paternity and have his name legally changed to Bibby. There was no question that he is my biological son. Ironically enough, about five years later, when Christie again became pregnant, I was informed that the second child could be mine or someone else's biologically. Christie asked if I wanted to take responsibility for this child and give him my name. Of course, I agreed. I was very excited to have another child.

So, when Matthew David Bibby was born, I got the privilege to sign his birth certificate. He is a Bibby boy through and through. I'll make one admission in reference to Christie: she is a better pilot than I am, but only by a little. The main thing is that we both love our boys and grandkids very much. Christie and I still never have a crossword, and I happily report that she is married to a great guy. We all love Eddie, and they are happy and thriving.

Then came Karen Gayle. I met Karen Gayle through my line of work. She had an abusive husband who was a substance abuser, and as a certified outreach specialist, I often got calls such as this. The husband was facing some legal issues, and Karen had three young kids, so she needed some guidance on how to navigate what she was going through. The day I met her, I told her it would require some effort on my part to be professional because I was very attracted to her. I don't think it scared her; instead, I think she was flattered.

We became friends, and almost thirty years later, Karen and I hold the record for the most times we split up and got back together. We almost got legally married a couple of times. We even went so far as to obtain a license once and had a place where the ceremony was going to be, but as always, we were all over the place emotionally. There was lots of love and intense attraction, but we were volatile. One of my favorite stories is when we were on the way to a 12-step meeting, and Karen got mad at me. I had no recollection of what it was about. She reminded me it was about a woman, of course.

She got so angry that she pulled my ear so hard that she tore it away from my head. It bled like crazy. We have always laughed about when she got so mad that she almost tore my ear off. We had great times. We kissed alongside the Rhine River in Cologne, Germany. We danced in a club in Istanbul, Turkey, and we fed and watered horses on the farm where we lived.

All that we did was fun, exciting, and often fiery. I'm proud to report that Karen is doing well. She is very involved in a strong spiritual journey and is crushing it, and her daughter Hope is a shining star who is very precious to us all.

Victoria Lanell was married when we first met. We met through a mutual friend. We'd all been in prison, and we had that common bond. Vicky and her husband Rick were in recovery for addiction, so there was that. We developed a good friendship. After she divorced, she was selling mobile homes in Waco, and I started going down to see her. She was a hot, wild redhead.

*What's not to like about that?*

After our relationship heated up, we wore out the roads, getting together between Waco and Fort Worth. Shortly before we started living together, we took a trip to Louisiana to gamble. I had a really good night at the tables. While at the casino, I did something I had never done and haven't since—I bought Vicky a $9 cup of fancy coffee. We left the casino with me, having won $3,800. We drove home and went to Walmart, buying a bunch of stuff we didn't need. Vicki says she still has much of it. It was fun.

The next day was a Sunday, and Vicki had to go back to work. I rented a limousine and drove her from Fort Worth to Waco to her work in the limo. When we arrived at her work, we were both standing up through the roof, waving at the people she worked with.

When I got back to Fort Worth, I picked up my oldest son in the limo, and we went to a Dallas Cowboys game. He cared very little about the football game, but he enjoyed the limo.

Shortly after that, Vicki moved in with me, and we were together uninterrupted for eight and a half years. We had a very good partnership. She became my travel manager, and at that time, I was traveling a lot. We went to Europe several times, to LA, and to New York many times. All I had to do was show up and perform. Vicki pretty much took care of everything else.

One time, we were in a subway in New York. I didn't even know the name of our hotel. She was looking at a subway map at a stop and suddenly stood up.

"Get off here," she said.

She stepped off, the door shut, and off I went on the subway without her. I was wondering, what the hell am I going to do now? Two stops down, as I was pondering where to get off, she stepped back on. She had caught up with me and got back on the same train I was on.

I told her, "Don't ever do that to me again."

She didn't.

We were coming home from a gig in Finland—me, Vicky, and Ken. We had a layover in Amsterdam. The weather in Europe was fine, but in the US, much of the country was socked in and experiencing a brutal winter storm, so we could not get home. We spent about two days in the Amsterdam airport before they finally got us out to Memphis. When we got to Memphis, it was going to be another day before we could get to DFW, our final destination. Because we were on an international flight, they had to provide us with rooms, meals, and transport.

We were waiting in line for our vouchers when Ken got the bright idea to tease Vicki.

"Vicki, before you started coming along, we never had these kinds of problems," he said.

It did not sit well with the redheaded hillbilly from Arkansas. She told Ken, with about thirty people listening and in way more colorful vernacular than I will use, "Until you can do for Jackie what I can do for him, I'll be coming on these trips whether you do or not."

It was tense for a little while, but thank goodness they made up before we went to bed that night.

One time, we were on a flight from Las Vegas to Dallas. At the time, Randall Cunningham was playing quarterback for the Dallas Cowboys. When we boarded the plane, he was sitting in first class. I recognized him and got very excited that we were on the same flight.

"I wish I could get my picture made with him," I said.

About halfway through the flight, it was kind of quiet, and the stewards were way in the back.

Vicky said, "Let me out."

"Where are you going?" I asked.

"I'm going to talk to Randall Cunningham," she answered.

"You can't go up there," I replied.

"What are they going to do? Kick me off the airplane?" She raised her eyebrow.

A few minutes later, she came back and said, "He'll be waiting for us at the gate."

And he was. We got pictures and met his wife and kids. They were in the back with us. Turns out kids can't ride in first class.

We had many amazing adventures. We are great friends to this day, and we speak on the phone every few days. When I'm in the area where she lives, I'm often a guest in her home. I even had the pleasure of officiating her son's wedding.

When I met Alyssa, she was twenty-four and I was sixty-five. She was a very petite, cute, redheaded nurse. I was friends with her mom, and she introduced us. Sparks flew pretty fast, and within a couple of weeks, I had her living with me. We were together for about two years. She tried to keep up with me, and she did a pretty good job, but I'm pretty active for an old dude.

Alyssa loved the snake shows and was a pretty big fan of attention herself. She learned to handle snakes pretty well and never had an accident—at least she never got herself bit.

At a show in Louisiana, she was walking around with a 12-foot Burmese python and somehow got a security guard bit. It was a non-venomous bite, but it did draw blood. That almost got me sued. I guess it could have cost me my snakes. I sure didn't have any money.

One day Alyssa asked, "Could we go to the pound?"

She wanted to adopt a small dog. When we got to the pound, it didn't take long for her to fall in love with a black pit bull that weighed about sixty-five pounds. We named him Cesar Augustus Bibby. I didn't really want a dog, but I loved Cesar. He was a fine dog. Now, he rests peacefully in my backyard under a pecan tree.

I'm proud to report that Alyssa is doing well. She is remarried and has two beautiful daughters that I'm sure will be firecrackers just like their mom. I don't really get why people get divorced and hate their exes. I love and respect every one of my exes. They're all fine women and deserve all the best. They all treated me way better than I deserved. I even got along pretty well with all of my husband-in-laws.

In a nutshell, I have been blessed to have known some incredible women in my life. Each one has taught me something valuable and left a lasting impact on my heart. I love and respect every one of them and wish them all the best.

Now, having shared almost all about the women in my life, let's move to God's second gift—*food.*

I guess I became aware of my addiction to food when I realized that I fantasized about food. Some of you know how it is: you finish a good meal, you're stuffed and completely satisfied, and you start thinking about what you're going to eat next and where you're going to eat the next meal. My favorite place to eat, no contest, is Mary's Cafe in Strawn, Texas. I love the owner, the staff, the ambiance, and the food. We have filmed there several times and brought rattlesnake meat, which she cooks and gives out as free samples to her diners. Mary and I are lifelong friends and always will be. I'll be eating with her frequently for as long as I'm able.

I like most all foods except seafood. I don't like anything that comes out of the ocean unless it's wearing a bathing suit. But my favorite ethnic food has always been German food, usually schnitzel. One of my favorite German food restaurants is Ava's in Lampasas. They have two of my promo pics on the ceiling, and that's always nice.

Of course, the Idle Rich Pub in Fort Worth is always worth the trip. I like Mexican food, especially Tex-Mex. *Who doesn't?*

I'm not a big fan of Italian, though. That's my son Michael's favorite food. He traveled with me to Italy to do a TV show, and he couldn't wait to try traditional Italian food.

It was bland, and he said, "This ain't no Olive Garden."

There are many good eating places in Texas, but not many that I haven't tried at least once or twice. I have to mention Lowake Steakhouse in Rowena. You can have a great $30 steak there. The Pearl Cactus in Blanket, Texas, is indeed a gem, but the steaks are to die for, even though it's a little out of my pay grade. It's great for a special occasion.

Now, I can cook myself, but of course, eating out is more my style. I'm a country cook, not many courses. If you get an entree and a veggie, I'm on fire. It's usually a meat dish and some bread. I mentioned my oldest boy is into Italian, while my youngest boy Matthew—if it's not chicken, it's not for him. It's for sure all the Bibby boys love to eat.

My love for food is still strong, and I continue to enjoy the culinary delights that life has to offer. I look forward to many more adventures and meals in the years to come.

# Chapter Eight

## Other Characters

I perceive myself as a character in my own story, shaped by a steady stream of other characters. When I was young, I was shy and often felt embarrassed, thinking I wasn't as good as those around me.

I remember in the seventh grade, my dad noticed my insecurity and told me, "You have two arms and two legs just like everybody else. You can do anything they can do."

At that time, that statement was true. I had a lot of friends, though I struggled with my closest ones—Carl, Robert, Richard. If I mentioned one of my best friends, would it offend someone else, like Timbo? I did have many great buddies, and we spent the night together and hung out.

The struggle continued into my adult life. When Robert and Susie got married, they asked me to be their best man. I was happy and proud. So, when I married, I should have asked Robert to be my best man, but I chose the easier way. I didn't have a best man, aiming to avoid hurt feelings.

I had many great friends in my early life. Carl, Robert, Richard, Tim, Kenneth, Grant, Danny, the Snake Handlers—

Dougie, Ken, Michael, and Terry—Landon, Brit, Robert. Later came Kirk, Donny, Scott, Marty, Justin, Paul, Jimmy, Todd, Jared, and then the ladies—Vicky, Karen Shai, Betty, JJ, Kaylie, Jessica, Felicia, Allison, and more.

Then there was Barry and Joe from my autism roundup, Charlie, Annie, Tracy, and Billy. With all these characters impacting my life, I might forget to mention some. These stories are not in any particular order or sequence; each anecdote stands on its own merit.

Dr. Ratan was a dear friend from Cisco, Texas, in 2004. Dr. Ratan was my college English professor during my first college attempts in 1969, 1970, and 1971. He also taught me during my second college attempt in the late 1980s and early 1990s. We often visited and talked about everything under the sun. He was brilliant and wrote a well-received piece about me for Texas Magazine. He passed away in 2023. I miss him; he was one of my mentors and my hero.

Kirk Arnold and Marvelous Mel were two of my forever friends. I called Kirk "Captain Kirk." We were roommates for almost three years while I attended Tarleton State University and Kirk and I worked for the treatment center, Summer Sky. We were like the odd couple and liked to tell the story of what led to our divorce. One of our friends, Pamela Kay Phillips, whom we called PK, stayed at our house overnight. The next day, she made a chicken salad sandwich and left the dirty bowl in the sink. Kirk and I had an unwritten agreement about leaving dishes in the sink. When he saw the bowl, he assumed I was responsible and said something. I didn't even know what he was talking about. Our discussion escalated into a fight.

We broke a chair, knocked out a sheetrock wall, and fought to a draw. I left, came back later, and fought some more. Kirk told me later that he had never had anyone hit him that hard. He moved out, and it took a couple of weeks before we made up. We became ride-or-die friends until his passing. I had the honor of officiating his celebration of life.

Marvelous Mel was good friends with Victoria; they spent time together. When Mel was paroled, she moved into our spare bedroom. When Kirk went through a divorce, he wound up on our couch. We were all thick as thieves. Vicki and I often walked in the early morning before work.

One morning, on our walk, she informed me, "Kirk and Mel are doing the dance with no pants."

I was shocked. I thought I would have known. It turned out that one night, after they watched a movie, Mel stood up, turned around, and reached out to Kirk, informing him he wasn't sleeping on the couch anymore. He moved into Mel's room. They later married but were together from that night until Kirk passed.

*Go, Marvelous Mel*

I met Paul Hyde by walking into his office many years ago when I worked for Summer Sky. Paul became my attorney, friend, mentor, and advisor.

When he says, *'I got you,'* he means it.

He's one of the best fathers, attorneys, businessmen, and guitar players I've ever met. Several years ago, we had a tattoo party.

Paul said, "Tattoo my logo on your back, wherever, and I'll be on retainer to you for life."

I did, and he has. He has been involved in a few snake escapades, but I'll let him tell you about that.

Another very dear and invaluable friend I met while working for Summer Sky is Christie Hitchcock. She is a probation officer in Hamilton, Texas. A lovely lady inside and out, Christie has a few tattoos and wears them well. She has two beautiful daughters, now all grown up, but I met them when they were young.

One day, Christy shared with me that some kids at school had told her girls they didn't know me. So, we made a plan to visit the school. I would have lunch with her daughters, and everything was going great. Some of the kids even asked to take a picture with me.

When one of the girls came up to get her picture taken, Christie's daughter said, "Oh no, no, you can't get your picture taken with Mr. Bibby. You're the one who said you didn't know him."

One of my greatest stories involves my Bibby boys, Michael and Matthew. We lived in Whiskey Flats, just outside of Fort Worth. My boys were young—Michael was about 11, and Matthew was 6. Anyway, I had two cobras living in a shoebox inside my living room, with a lock on the box to keep them secure. What I didn't know was that my young boys knew a combination of the lock. Years later, I discovered that when I wasn't around, they would often bring all the kids in the neighborhood over, unlock the box, and show them the cobras. It's a miracle nobody got killed.

I don't recall the day I met Shai Berry, but it feels like I've known her forever. God doesn't make better friends than Shai. She appreciates what I do and is my self-proclaimed publicist. She has made it her task to ensure that lots of people know me and give me work to do. I wish I had a bunch of money; I'd give Shea some of it. She has worked tirelessly for me and never asked for a dime. One of our stories involves a mutual friend, Zach Webb. I was playing a gig in Brownwood, Texas, many years ago, and Zach and his partner performed that day.

I was impressed and told Shea, "Check this guy out. I think there's something there."

She did, and she is now his manager. They're killing it with albums, singles, and gigs all over the U.S. Congratulations to them both. I love them.

Dr. Gus Gross is a premier expert on venomous bites in Texas, probably in the nation, and on the short list of experts in the world. Gus knows I'm anything but a scientist, but he's allowed me to be involved in a couple of his scientific papers. It's a great honor. We traveled together to Oxford, England, where he presented a paper on the bite that cost me my leg.

The paper was titled "Size Matters," and he let me do most of the handling on a study about the correlation between the distance between the fangs and the length of a rattlesnake.

Gus does a lot of work with first responders and medical personnel, and he often lets me talk a little about what it's like to be bitten by a venomous animal. I love Dr. Gus Gross; he's a valuable friend to have. I'm a ballsy kind of guy and a macho man if you will, but my next friend puts me to shame, and he's not even a daredevil. He's a science guy. My friend Bobby Stevens from Ranger, Texas, has developed what is known as hyper immunity to venom—hemotoxin and neurotoxin. He has been self-injecting venom compounds for years, and let me assure you, he has proved his point. A few years ago, we produced a huge event with big names like Doug Supernaw, and as part of the event, Bobby went on stage in front of about 5,000 people and took a cobra bite to his forearm. He walked away with no treatment and no long-term damage. I salute you, Bobby. Big ones, my friend. Big ones.

Gotta give a shout-out to my core four, the fabulous five. You'll see them mentioned throughout my story, but in no way can I do justice to the miles and experiences we've shared over forty years. So, I salute Doug, Michael, Ken, and Terry. Yeah, we rock.

If you've known me for more than thirty minutes, you've seen me take my shirt off to show my tattoos. I've had work done all over the place, but my happy spot for skin art is Insane Ink in Early, Texas. Nobody does it better than Jerry Crouch and his crew. They're the best of the best.

There's something about these tattoos. I don't know what it is. These tattoos are like Lay's potato chips: you can't have just one, and I'm never done. I only have 67 tattoos so far. Most people know I have a savior complex. I love to throw my cape down for a person in distress, so I get lots of contacts asking for my help. Most go nowhere, although I try to evaluate each one on its own merit. One of the most interesting and long-lasting friendships came from such a contact.

My friend Jessica Graham, whose last initial has changed because she recently married, is doing oh so well. She was in jail in Abilene and found my name and number in a book.

She called me, and we started talking. I helped her get out of jail and into a recovery house. She got a job, and when it was time for her to be picked up and taken home, that was over five years ago. We're close friends to this day.

I never professed to be the best snake handler or hunter, but over the years, I've hunted with some of the best—Larry Lee, Jim Bob Bassham, and Jesse Cantu, Harley Tyler and his wife Joy, And Taylor Throckmorton the best artifact hunter that I know. One of my hunting buddies is Willie Mosley. We've hunted, done shows, trained dogs, and sometimes I even listen to him play music. His wife is a probation officer. Years ago, I was in a probation office working for Summer Sky when a nice lady came out, and started glaring at me.

She said, "I know who you are. You're the man who made my husband think he should hunt rattlesnakes."

Thankfully, she lost her anger.

Another dear friend I met under unconventional circumstances is my very little but very loud ride-or-die, Amber Dawn. When we met several years ago, she was incarcerated. A mutual friend told her about me, and we hit it off quickly. I was impressed by her understanding of recovery. If ever there was a poster girl for recovery, it's her—very pretty, exceptionally intelligent, with tons of potential and talent. But like many of us, a real drug addict, she made some poor choices when she was young, which cost her dearly.

What impressed me about her is her commitment to her children. She has been back in society for just over a year. She works hard, doing all she can to raise her kids. She's getting an education and intends to work to help others like us. A very noble passion, my friend. It's not easy to get along with her, but neither am I.

We talk about pretty much everything. I trust Amber, and I think she trusts me too. Amber's a bit of a B-word sometimes, but I think it's kind of cute. She's one of the miracles that recovery has brought into her life. Some things she could not do for herself, but she's made great strides on her own. It is my honor to watch her learn and grow.

*Go ahead with your bad self, Amber. You got this!*

I have another friend, Peggy, a retired school teacher. We went through school together for all 12 years. Peggy is pretty and smart and has always been popular. We were both raised in the Church of Christ. We've always stayed in touch, and she has encouraged me to write a book more than anyone else. I appreciate her vote of confidence. I hope she is not disappointed.

It's a small world in recovery. I did an intervention on a young man and sent him to Summer Sky where I was working. His name is Scott Kelly. A few years later, he bought the place, and I ended up working for him for years. He's a good boss. In the herpetology community, I'm not the most loved guy around. It's well known that much of my journey has involved rattlesnake roundups—events that are much hated by most herpetologists.

But I've been blessed to make friends with some of the big names in the herp community. One such friend is Tom Crutchfield. Tom is no snowflake; he calls it like he sees it and pulls no punches. He's very educated and intelligent, and he has enough common sense to know that none of us are all right or all wrong.

Tom and I have been communicating for several years. I respect him, and I know we have a lot of common interests. He knows way more about his animals than I do about mine. Although we don't agree on all points, I value his opinion and knowledge, and I appreciate his willingness to discuss things with me and allow me to learn at my ripe old age. I'm still teachable.

I wish to give a shout-out to some other herpetologists I trust and respect: Danny Mendez, Kelly Hill, and Todd Autry. All of them have helped me on my journey.

During junior high, we had a couple of new kids move in: Debbie Kay and Danny Ray. Our math teacher, Mr. Watkins, was also the principal, so he had to get them checked in at our school. He left our math class unattended while he went across the hall to get them checked in. Every boy in our class had to sharpen his pencil a time or two so we could peer across the hall and check out these new kids. Debbie Kay was not at all hard to look at, so she was very well-received in our class. She was smart, had a good sense of humor, and was pretty, so of course, she was popular.

The next year, in eighth grade, we had a party at my house. We were asking girls to walk around the house with us. I was plenty nervous, but I asked Debbie Kay. Well, it was not my first kiss, but it was definitely a few pay grades above any kisses I'd had before. I got two kisses and was on cloud nine. I later heard she kissed James Gerheart that night too.

Was I upset? Lord, no. I was just excited to have been on the shortlist. Debbie later married the star quarterback, Danny White. We called him Booney. They had a couple of fine boys who went on to become coaches and superstars. Oh, one thing I should mention: Danny was our quarterback on our football team, and I was his center. So, I'm sad to report that he put his hands between my legs way more than anybody else did throughout high school.

I'm an active member of the Cross Texas Cowboy Church. I am ordained and serve as a second associate pastor. I get to read the announcements and events and occasionally bring the message. I love my fellowship. It's a fine group of sinners who are blessed to be active Christians. Our pastor is Marty Bingham, an old farmer and bull rider who had quite a journey before he came back to the Lord. His wife, Debbie, like most pastor's wives, works twice as hard as Marty. Debbie is an inspiration to us all. She works tirelessly and serves the Lord at our church. Our other associate pastor, James, also has a checkered past but is a pillar of our fellowship today. James has a great wife, Jenny, who also works hard to see our fellowship thrive.

I met JJ several years ago. Little did I know she would become one of my ride-or-die friends and that I would come to love her, her family, and even some of her animals. She has more critters than most zoos. Her husband and two kids are like family to me. If JJ is your friend, you don't have to wonder where she stands or where you stand with her if you need her. She's never wavering. If you want to know about keeping animals, this girl knows her stuff.

*Thanks, JJ. You're a crackerjack!*

Having a good doctor is a huge blessing, and I sure have the cream of the crop. Dr.Guile P., as I call him, grew up in my community. I'm close friends with him and his parents, and I love his nurses, Davidie and Debbie Kay. He loves to tell the story about all the snakes I've shown him over the years.

One of his favorites is about a big old cobra that I had. It's hilarious when he tells the story. Guile takes good care of me. I think I might live to be a hundred, but at least till I'm in my nineties.

I met Todd Skinner and his wife several years ago. Todd and I worked together. He's the real deal—genuine as it gets. He has more hustle in his left foot than most people have in their whole body. I stay as a guest with very few people, but I do stay with his family in South Texas. Randall Briggs in Paris,

Texas, is the biggest buyer of rattlesnakes in Texas and Oklahoma by far. He makes the highest quality snake skin products on the market, and you can count on Randall to do what he says and say what he does.

Kelly Freeman, also known as Tootie Fruite, is a dear friend of mine. She has battled many demons in her life, but she's currently on a strong spiritual journey. I'm sure she will be a powerful influence in many people's lives.

Texas Dog Academy is run by Bill Walters and his wife, Rita, and daughter, Gabbie. They provide everything having to do with dogs. We've been doing snake-proofing clinics for over twenty years. Many people have dogs that could potentially encounter venomous snakes. Dogs are curious and will go to investigate, often getting bitten. We milk the snake to remove most of the venom, then place sutures over the fangs to hold them in place. This way, the snake cannot inject venom. We let the dog discover the snake—see, smell, and hear it—then we shock the dog. This teaches the dog to leave the snakes alone.

Timmy Bryce Johnson, or Timbo as we call him, is my lifelong friend. We played in the dirt together and were always around each other growing up. We were not above playing tricks on each other, especially at certain times of the year. Here in Central Texas, we see a lot of tarantula spiders crossing the road. One evening, myself, Carl, Robert, and Chi were on a mission. We caught and put those spiders in a beef jerky jar. I think we caught about eight of them. As it was getting dark, we had to figure out what to do with our critters.

Timbo had a nice gold Chevy pickup with a manual four-speed on the floor. We saw him and blinked him down. I parked behind him so my associates could get a clear view of what I was doing. I had my jar down low and walked up to his window.

"Turn on the interior light. I want to show you something," I said.

He did, and I twisted the top off my jerky jar and poured eight huge tarantulas into Timbo's lap. He almost killed me getting out of his pickup, and we all spent about an hour getting all the spiders before he would get back in.

Many years ago, I met Allison Jones at an NA meeting. After the meeting, she was passing out flyers asking for work mowing lawns. I flirted with her a little, thinking, *'She can mow my lawn anytime. She's cute.'*

Little pixie, maybe five feet tall. She was smart and always full of energy. We developed a close bond very quickly and have traveled many miles together without ever having a crossword. She was with me in Dallas when I received a bite that cost me my leg. She took on a lot of responsibility that weekend.

She persevered and did well. I'm the current director of the Roatch Foundation, a 501(c)(3) nonprofit that provides information and transportation for people struggling with addictive disorders and their friends and families. We are primarily subsidized by Linda and Arnold R., a couple of friends of mine who have been blessed financially and wanted this nonprofit to provide help to those in need. We're doing some very effective work. Thank you, Linda and Arnold. We're just getting started.

Ms. Pamela Phillips, or PK as I call her, is my dear friend and a retired school counselor. We became friends when I started doing lectures at her school on drug abuse. We've stayed friends through her career in three different schools now. She's also a producer of a radio show, and I can't wait to be a guest on her show.

Felicia Dawn Andrews is another friend I'm grateful for. No surprise, we bonded over having the same first name as my mom. This beautiful lady has a pure, sensitive, and kind soul, though it's wrapped up in a rough exterior. Felicia has a lot of tattoos, most of them dark, but she's always the first on the scene if anybody in her social circle is in need. I have very few friends with whom I share as many common interests as I do with Felicia. We can talk for days, but sometimes our agendas are opposed. I can assure you, though, that when the knives come out, I'm cutting for Felicia, and I know she'll do the same for me. And if all else fails, we'll just go get a tattoo.

If you're in a dark alley late at night, you don't want to encounter my next friend, Jared "Big Boots" Hogget. He's big, and he looks mean. I'm betting he can be, if called for, but he has a heart of gold. He's one of the best mechanical geniuses I've ever known. He's bailed my tail feathers out of the fire more times than I can count. If you don't need your car or motorcycle fixed, he can sing you a mighty fine song, many of which he wrote.

I was at the pharmacy getting a prescription filled when I saw a stunning redhead with several visible tattoos. I tried hard not to get caught staring, but I couldn't keep my eyes off of her. Soon, I could no longer resist. I complimented her on her skin art. She was very friendly, and I guess we would have talked all day if our meds hadn't been ready. This good-looking redhead was Kaylie Donica.

I managed to give her a card with my cell phone number on it. We made contact, and it was only a few days before we went on our first date. Kaylee had just had hip surgery and used a walker, but that was no deterrent to my taking her to a Donnie Evans II concert for our first date. We were an item for several years. She remains one of my most trustworthy friends. She's married to a fine man now, and she obviously has a type because her husband and I could pass for brothers.

It's hard for me to recall a time when I didn't know Ken Darnell. I've been working with snakes as a hobby for over fifty years, and I believe he was around when I got started. Ken is a patent attorney, and we call him the Venom Gypsy. I think I can safely say no one has extracted more venom from more places and more animals than my friend Ken. He's one of the smartest men I know, but he can be a little abrasive at times. He gets annoyed when people spread information that he knows is not true. Ken has been very involved in developing medicines that use venom. He can be a great guy; he just doesn't suffer fools gladly.

Thomas Alman and his wife, Tracy, are some good people. I know Thomas doesn't much care for the politics that go on at roundups, so he has been giving me his snakes for years. For a guy who's forgotten more about catching snakes than most hunters will ever know, Thomas is old school and as honest as they come.

My friends Robert and Susie Clark are lifelong friends. I've already mentioned that I was the best man at their wedding. They honored me by making me godfather to their son. I am not Catholic, but I assure you I take this title and responsibility very seriously. Doug and Carla are my mouse connection. They have thousands of mice, so I buy most of my snake food from them. I hate feeding snakes; I always feel sorry for the mice.

Concluding, there are so many more characters I have encountered in my life. But I cant fit all of them in this book, let alone in this chapter. So, to some of you, I'm giving a shout out.

Landon Shults, Haley Rains, Rattlesnake Cowboy, Nick Dames, Amy Harry Glavin, and Brit Stevens, I remember you guys too.

My final salute in this section goes to Jimmy Hughes, a guy I love like family. I've sponsored him for many years, and our journey has definitely been a two-way street. So, let's keep on learning, my friend.

Now, I know many of you will be attending my funeral. Some of you who don't will miss an event. I have a pretty cool ending plan. As an ordained minister, I'm often asked to do funerals. Being the attention seeker that I am, I came up with the idea: why not preach my own funeral?

So, my son, who does a lot of my shooting and editing for my YouTube channel, will film me doing my own celebration of life. It will be played at my funeral. I plan to be cremated. Half my ashes will be interred in our family plot, and the other half will be scattered over Rising Star from an airplane. This honor has been agreed to by my dear friend and attorney, Mr Paul Hyde.

The more I think of the people who got magically woven with my life, their impact, and their influence, the more grateful I become, even for having them closer. Friends who always stood beside me, mentors who devoted their lives to my betterment, or unsung heroes—they all contributed to making me who I am today.

With their unwavering support, we have shared experiences beyond counting, and each of them brings qualities by which this journey became enriched in ways that words can never express. The chapter then rejoices in ever-supporting presences and in deep relationships that kept me afloat through life's many ups and downs, to friendships that stood the test of time, and to bonds that continue to inspire and uplift me high up.

# Chapter Nine

# Performance Art

If I could be anything I wanted, there's no question about it—I'd be an actor. Hands down. No hesitation. I've always felt like I could do it well. Maybe it's just a dream, but I hope I'm not delusional. I mentioned earlier that my first role as an actor was playing Elvis upon *'Reflection.'* I need to reconsider that statement.

My first role was actually way back in the fourth grade. I played *Amerigo Vespucci*, the explorer America was named after. My mom made me this great outfit, complete with a cardboard sword covered in tinfoil. I was so proud of that costume.

After that, my next role was as *Elvis* in a parade. Then, I had a supporting role in my senior play. I guess I was unknowingly building my acting resume early on.

My first television appearance was in the early seventies on a regional program called *'The Sylvia Chalet Show,'* a talk show where I discussed being a snake hunter and my experience competing in rattlesnake sacking contests. That was a wild experience, and it was just the beginning.

My first agent was Peggy Taylor, from a talent agency out of Dallas. I had a great time with that group, but in those days, I wasn't the most responsible person.

Now, I chuckle, shaking my head at the irony.

The only job they ever booked me for was a beer commercial, and guess what? I missed the gig because I was in jail. Oh, the irony of that.

At the time, Peggy was also representing Hollywood Henderson. I was really impressed by that. Years later, he and I became friends. We even worked together at the same treatment center. Hollywood is a really cool guy with some incredible stories.

My first national TV appearance came on *'The Chevy Chase Show.'* What a blast that was! I got to show Chevy how to milk a rattlesnake and even gave him a snakeskin cap. I bet he still has that cap somewhere.

During that trip, I met Jamie Lee Curtis—an incredibly beautiful person, and very kind. I also met Sam Elliott, another genuinely nice man. And Chevy? He was really cool, too.

Looking back on my journey, I've been involved in a lot of big-budget projects and had the pleasure of working with some of the biggest names in the business. But I guess my main claim to fame is the reality show *'Rattlesnake Republic.'* It ran on Animal Planet for three seasons. In case you're not aware, reality TV is only loosely based on reality. It's very much an acting job, and I loved every second of it. I would do it again in a heartbeat.

Right after *'The Chevy Chase Show,'* I decided to take my acting seriously. I enrolled in an acting school and signed with *'Spotlight Talent Agency.'* Sharon Campbell, the agent I worked with, taught me a lot. I went on a lot of auditions and actually landed a few jobs.

Let me give you a few highlights…

Feature films including *'Courage Under Fire'* with Denzel Washington, *'Michael,'* with John Travolta, *'Keys to Tulsa'* with Mary Tyler Moore, *'Any Given Sunday'* with Al Pacino, *'Slap Her,' 'She's French!'* with Piper Perabo, *'Serving Sara,'* and *'Just a Little bit Crazy*

Then there were made-for-TV movies, including 'Deadly Family Secrets' with Loni Anderson, *'The Unspoken Truth'* and *'America's Dream'* with Danny Glover, *'To Serve and Protect,'* and *'Streets of Laredo'* with James Garner.

Pilots I've been in include *'Depraved,' 'Runaway Heart,' and 'Party Girl.'*

Now, moving on to episodic television. Well, I've done *Kindit* for Dutch television, *'Don't Try This at Home'* for British television, two episodes of *'Guinness Primetime'* on Fox, *two shows* in Germany, *'The Tonight Show'* on NBC, *'Zone'* in Finland, two episodes of *'Ripley's Believe It or Not,'Sensless Acts of Video* on MTV, *'The Burton Gilliam Show,' 'You Asked For It'* on NBC, *'Viva Variety'* on Comedy Central, *'Maury Povich'* on CBS, *'Austin Stories'* on MTV, *'Walker,' 'Texas Ranger'*—I did two episodes *'Skyjacked and Blue Movies.*

And let's not forget Steve Harvey's *'Big Time Challenge'* and *'The Go-Big Show'* with Snoop Dogg. Oh, and I have three YouTube channels, too.

I had a very successful run with *Performance Talent Agency* with Kaylynn Scott.

I remember during one of our training sessions, she told a room full of actors, "I wish you were all like Jackie Bibby. He thinks he's going to get every job he goes up for."

And you know what? She was right!

I have no doubt about my ability to do any job in the acting profession. I've had starring roles in feature films and lots of speaking parts in film and TV projects, but if someone asks me to be an extra on a project that I think has merit, I'll do it in a heartbeat. I've never met a camera I didn't love, and I'm always fascinated anytime I'm on set.

I've met an unbelievable group of people in my pursuit and interest in performance art. One of those people is Becky McCants, also known as Rebecca Moore. We met in acting school in the early nineties. I think our journeys have run somewhat parallel. We've traveled a long distance together, worked on projects together, supported each other by attending events, and done training together. If I ever have the money to fund some of my projects, she'll definitely be considered my co-star in anything that she fits.

To Rebecca, I want to say, *keep on reading, Rebecca. One or both of our big breaks might be just around the corner!*

About thirty years ago, I found myself working for a small local television station out of Granbury, Texas. During this time, I crossed paths with a man who would leave a lasting impression on me—Charlie Throckmorton. Charlie was a seasoned rodeo announcer, and his passion for the community was infectious.

One day, he suggested I get involved with an organization he was deeply committed to—*The Bobby Norris Roundup for Autism*. The cause seemed both fun and profoundly meaningful, so I jumped in with both feet and have been involved ever since.

At that time, autism was a term I knew little about. I didn't know anyone who was autistic, but the cause resonated with me. Fast forward to today, and I have a ten-year-old grandson who is autistic—one of the brightest lights in my life. It sure feels like a divine wink from above, reminding me that I was meant to be part of this incredible journey.

Over the years, my involvement with the Roundup has introduced me to some remarkable people. Bobby Norris and his wife, JJ, have hearts as big as Texas itself. I've met actor Barry Corbin and his lovely wife, Jo, as well as actress Annie Lockhart and her two amazing kids.

Dean Smith, an actress, stuntman, and Olympic gold medalist, became a cherished friend, as did his son, Finus Smith, who has now made his mark in the music industry. Tracy Shakespeare, a model, actress, and true horsewoman, also joined this incredible circle. The list could go on, but it's clear that this is a group of extraordinary individuals committed to an extraordinary cause.

One of the more interesting characters I've met through this journey is Valerie Fillmore, affectionately known as *'Snake Chick.'* Valerie sports a tattoo of a rattlesnake that wraps around her body, starting at her foot and ending at her shoulder.

We first met when she played my ex-wife in an episode of 'Rattlesnake Republic,' and later in one of my YouTube videos. She was one of the most beloved characters on the show, not because she tried to be funny, but simply because she was being herself.

Ironically, Leroy wasn't even supposed to be in the show. The original cast member, Randall Briggs, got cold feet during filming, and I had to find a replacement fast. I knew just the person.

I went to Leroy's merchandise booth and asked, "Leroy, do you want to be on a TV show?"

He looked at me, grinned, and said, "Sure!"

And just like that, a star was born. Leroy was a natural, and from that day until the show was canceled, he became an integral part of *Rattlesnake Republic*.

In 2004, Dr. Cle Ratan wrote an article about me that was published in Texas Magazine. A guy from Houston, Graydon Taylor, read the article and reached out to me.

We became fast friends and business associates, collaborating on many projects over the years.

Graydon is an incredibly talented producer, actor, writer, and published author. I'm proud to call him my friend. He's the kind of guy who would go to the ends of the earth for you, no questions asked.

These days, there aren't many people interested in learning how to handle snakes. It's a dying art, but there's hope on the horizon. I've recently met a young couple, Nate and Rayleigh Reed, who are absolutely on fire for snake handling. Watching them grow, learn, and put their skills into action has been an absolute joy and privilege. They're stars in the making, and I can't wait to see where their journey takes them.

One of my dear friends, Todd Franco, is currently going through a tough time. He has a rare disease that has taken away much of his ability to move. We call him *Trapper Todd* because of his love for trapping and training dogs. Todd ran a business relocating nuisance animals for people who wanted them gone but didn't want them killed—a true blessing for both the animals and the people.

Thankfully, his son, Colton, has stepped up to continue the business while Todd focuses on his recovery. We're all hoping and praying for a speedy recovery for Trapper Todd.

Another close friend of mine is Jet Eller, an independent filmmaker from North Carolina. We've never met in person, but we've been friends for over a decade. We often discuss our shared obsession with filmmaking. Jet has made three or four films, one of which, *'Night Feeders,'* was a pretty good success. Many years ago, he wrote a screenplay called *'Pump House,'* which involves some rattlesnakes. If I ever come into any money, you can bet this picture show will get made.

During the filming of *Rattlesnake Republic*, Dougie, Michael, and I formed one team, while Robert Ackerman and Sean Jonas formed another. On the show, we were often portrayed as being in conflict with each other, but in reality, we had all worked together for years. Robert, in particular, was a wizard at getting the necessary paperwork for our international trips. He even got trapped in Istanbul, Turkey, for nine days once, just trying to get the right stamps to bring our snakes back into the United States.

*Talk about dedication!*

We were all incredibly competitive, which sometimes led to head-to-head challenges. I'll never forget our trip to California for Ripley's *'Believe It or Not.'* We did a bathtub sitting competition with rattlesnakes. Tiffany and Robert's team managed to get twenty-four rattlesnakes in the tub. Dougie and I, well, we got eighty-three. Of course, Dougie helped, but I was the one in the tub, so I'll take the credit for that win.

Another time, Robert set a world record for the most consecutive cobras kissed on the head. The hardest part of the stunt was actually getting enough cobras. We ordered sixty of them and had them shipped in. Robert did set the world record, but as fate would have it, someone with access to way more cobras than we did broke his record just a few months later. At least he held it for a little while.

Down in South Texas, near Beaumont, I have some friends who are into performance art. Garyand Shannon Sarge run a place called *'Gator Country.'* They also have a traveling show, and I've had the privilege of working with them both at their permanent venue and on the road. Their featured animals are gators, but they work with lots of different animals. Their show is exciting, fun, and very informative.

Closer to home, I have a couple of friends, Danny and Ruby Fisher, who have been part of my life since high school. Danny, like me, enjoys the limelight, but he found recognition differently. In his younger days, Danny was a world-class bodybuilder. He went to California and got in with some of the biggest names in the business.

He's a former Mr. Olympia and has won numerous other accolades. He even worked in Vegas as a gladiator at Caesar's Palace and had a role as Leatherface in one of the Star Trek movies. Danny's wife, Ruby, is a strong encourager of mine. Despite some health issues, she never complains.

Every time I see her and ask how she's doing, she responds with, "I can't complain to you. You never complain."

That strong affirmation means the world to me. Thank you, Ruby. I do try.

For those of you who followed *Rattlesnake Republic* closely, you might remember Riley Sawyer from Sweetwater, who was often portrayed as my enemy on the show. That was just for entertainment value—we were actually good friends. Sadly, Riley has since passed away. May he rest in peace. He was a super cool guy.

To give you an idea of how strong a medium television can be, consider this. Between the first and second seasons of the show, the interest and reach of our little production grew exponentially. We went from being a niche show to something much bigger, connecting with audiences far beyond our initial expectations.

And that's the thing about life—it's full of surprises, connections, and a circle of friends who become like family. From the rodeo announcer who introduced me to the Bobby Norris Roundup, to the snake-handling couple who are the future of the craft, to the filmmaker I've never met in person but consider a dear friend—every connection, every friendship, has added something unique and valuable to my journey.

I've been blessed in many ways throughout my life, but one of the greatest blessings has been the opportunity to observe and learn from remarkable people. Take Carol, for instance. Watching her carry her message of how to be a Christian has been nothing short of inspiring. She just keeps on keeping on, and I'm proud to be her cheerleader, rooting for her every step of the way.

In my journey, I've done a lot of radio, which means I've met more than my fair share of disc jockeys. Two of them have left a lasting impression on me. Mike Crow is one of them. I've followed him through so many radio stations that I've lost count. He's a great on-air personality, and he even appeared in one of my videos, *'Dodging Death.'* The other is Melissa K., a radio personality who always welcomes me onto her show. She knows how much I love to broadcast my exploits, especially at the Cross Texas Cowboy Church.

At that church, I met a man who has been a true inspiration, friend, and mentor to me: Justin Todd Herod. Most of you know that I'm most impressed by people who didn't get most of their message from a book. JTH, as I like to call him, is that kind of guy. He's the best preacher I've ever heard. He doesn't fit the mold of most preachers—he's buff, rough, and tatted up—but when he preaches or sings, the love of the Lord and his fellow Christians just drips off of him.

He may not like my snakes, but he loves me, and our friendship has enhanced the quality of my life in ways I can't fully express.

I could list all the awards and honors JTH has earned, but I suggest you go look him up, listen to a song or two, and you'll be a fan. I assure you of that. So far, he's released eleven albums, and I know he's not done yet. I would be remiss if I didn't mention his partner in all things, his beautiful wife, Rainie She glows just as brightly as JTH, and together, they are a true blessing to me.

I'm sure most of you have heard of Kevin Fowler. Well, I met him way back when almost nobody knew him. I was producing a rattlesnake show in Taylor, Texas, and he was the music headliner. I had never heard of him before, but he came down to our snake pit and hung out for a while. We did manage to get him in the pit, though he's no fan of rattlesnakes. As his career took off, many of our group stayed in touch with him. One of our events on the *Rattlesnake Republic* even featured him.

He has a hit song called *'Beer, Bait, and Ammo,'* so we called the event *Beer, Bait, and Rattlesnakes*. We managed to coax him back into the pit, and it was all being recorded. Ken Garrett, one of our snake handlers, ran a snake pinner up the back of Kevin's leg, and he nearly flew out of the pit! You can still see that video on his webpage. We're all big Kevin Fowler fans, and he always gives us a shout-out whenever he sees any of us at his concerts.

A few years ago, at a Scott Haley concert, I met a good-looking redheaded singer named Amelia Presley. After hearing her sing and seeing her perform, I was an instant fan. Imagine my surprise when we became friends, and she revealed to me that she wanted to learn how to handle rattlesnakes. Naturally, I was more than willing to oblige.

We've done several gigs together, and she's even appeared in some of my YouTube videos. Amelia is learning fast, and she brings a level of class to snake handling that I never could. We haven't done anything recently, but I know she's busy raising her talented, beautiful kids. I'm sure we'll work together again one of these days. And if you see her out performing somewhere, just know that the rattlesnake hat band she's wearing came from me.

*Sing on, my friend, sing on!*

So many people have touched my life and had an impact, both large and small. I've mentioned many of them here, but I know I've left some of you out. I'm sorry for that— it wasn't intentional. I'll try to get you in my next book.

Every encounter, every friendship, and every shared experience has shaped who I am today, and I'm eternally grateful for each one. Life's journey is filled with twists and turns, but it's the people we meet along the way who truly make it memorable.

# Chapter Ten

## One More Next

It was my junior year of high school after the last football game of the season. A crisp, cool night under the Texas stars. The adrenaline of the game was still in the air, but this time, it wasn't the glow of the stadium lights keeping us going. It was the flicker of a bonfire, the low hum of country music, and the laughter of friends that fueled us.

We were a bunch of kids out in the country, drinking beer and playing football in the dark. We didn't have a real football, but it didn't matter. We used a beer can instead. It was a night like so many others, where nothing mattered except being young and wild, with the freedom to dream as big as the Texas sky.

One of my friends turned to me at some point and asked, "Jackie, what do you think you'll do with your life?"

I didn't hesitate. I stood up straighter, took a swig of my beer, and said, "I'm going to be an actor, and I'm going to be famous."

The whole group burst out laughing, and I remember just grinning back. They thought it was funny, a pipe dream. But

I wasn't joking. After the laughter died down, we went back to our makeshift game, still kids in a world full of possibilities. That night, my friend might not have believed me, but I believed in myself. That was enough.

Years passed after high school. That friend moved away, like so many others from our small town. Life went on, and I lost track of him. Then, about thirty or forty years later, we crossed paths again. By that time, I'd done more in my life than I ever imagined back when we were kids playing with a beer can in the dirt.

We stood talking, catching up after so many years.

Out of nowhere, he said, "You know, Jackie, I remember what you said that night. You told us you'd be famous. And I've got to hand it to you. You made it. Almost everybody knows who you are. Every time I tell people I'm from Rising Star, they ask me, 'Do you know Jackie Bibby?'"

His words struck me. At that moment, I realized I had, in a way, done what I set out to do all those years ago. I made something of myself. If I were to die tomorrow, I'd have already far exceeded my wildest expectations. But just because I've achieved more than I ever imagined doesn't mean I'm done dreaming.

You see, I'm a creature of excess. 'Too much' is a phrase I've never really understood because it's never been enough for me. That hunger for more, that desire to push beyond what anyone thought possible—that's always been in my blood.

My ultimate dream? I want to write, produce, and star in a feature film. I want to tell stories that stir emotions, make people think, and leave a lasting impression. The kind of stories that, when the lights come up in the theater, the audience leaves a little different than when they arrived.

And I know I can do it. I've been on enough movie sets and paid attention to every detail, every process, like a sponge soaking up knowledge. No, I don't have formal training in filmmaking, but I've learned from experience.

With the right team by my side—people like Jet Ers, Donnie Evans II, and Grayden Taylor—I know we can make something special. Something that resonates.

*Magic will happen—I can feel it!*

And if you're reading this book, you're almost done with it. I hope you've enjoyed the ride. If you have, do me a favor— tell your family and friends about it. Spread the word. If this book sells well, who knows? Maybe I'll have the money to make that movie I've always dreamed of.

Imagine this. You're sitting in a movie theater someday, about to watch a feature film made by me. And you get to turn to the person next to you and say, "I helped this picture get made."

That's what keeps me going.

Now, I know some people might think I'm too old for such big dreams. After all, I'm seventy-three. But age has never been a limitation in my mind. I've still got plenty of irons in the fire. I'm running the Roatch Foundation, a 501(c)(3) nonprofit. I'm still doing snake shows. I'm training dogs to avoid rattlesnakes for about six kennels. I'm writing this book—and I'm sure I'll want to write another one or two after this.

So, surely, I can find time to make a movie or two. And, why not?

In fact, I've already got four movie projects in various stages of pre-production. The one that's closest to coming together is called *'Pump House'* by Jet Ers. It's a story based on an actual event—a man fell through the steps of his pump house, broke his leg, and couldn't get up. He had to lie there, surrounded by rattlesnakes, for two days until he was rescued.

Jet wrote an incredible screenplay around that event. It's a love story told in flashbacks, filled with suspense and heart. I'm set to play the role of the farmer, while Annie Lockhart, a well-known star of TV and film, will play my wife. Her daughter and my son will portray us as our younger selves.

Jet gave me the luxury of contributing to the script, which I appreciated. Let me share one of the scenes I suggested. It's a simple moment between Ray Storms, the farmer, and his wife, Doris. Ray sits down at the dining room table, watching Doris as she fills out sweepstakes entries.

He chuckles and says, "You're never going to win."

She looks up with a playful smile. "Well, I just might. I'm trying to win us a new pickup. And if I do, I might just give it to my young boyfriend."

Ray shakes his head, used to their banter. "Your young boyfriend, huh?"

That night, as they lie in bed, Ray snuggles close to Doris.

She opens her eyes wide and asks, "Ray, did you take one of those tablets?"

Ray grins and kisses her neck. "Well, with all that talk of young boyfriends, I thought I'd better protect my interests."

It's a bittersweet love story, one filled with humor and tenderness. But it's also about loss. Doris dies unexpectedly, and Ray finds himself trapped in the pump house, surrounded by rattlesnakes. It's in that isolation that he reflects on his life, his love for Doris, and whether or not he wants to go on living. The film will keep you on the edge of your seat, not just because of the snakes, but because of the raw emotion at its heart.

Another project I'm working on is inspired by my favorite song, *'Angel Flying Too Close to the Ground'* by Willie Nelson. This one's about recovery from addiction, a subject that's incredibly close to my heart. My original intent was to have my dear friend, Heather, play the co-starring role, but I've lost touch with her. Wherever she is, I hope and pray she's happy and thriving. In the meantime, my friend Amber is interested in the part, and I know she'll do it justice. This film's a real tear-jerker, filled with hope and redemption.

Then there's *'Close Enough to Perfect,'* a love story loosely wrapped in the tale of a utopian society. I've always envisioned two incredible actresses for the lead roles—Jodie Foster and Rebecca Moore. So, if either of you happens to be reading this, I've got the story, and if you've got the money, we could make something truly special.

And lastly, there's this quirky idea I've been toying with. It's about a high-level drug dealer who's on the brink of losing his wife and children because of his addiction. He gets busted and sent to prison, where he goes straight and starts to reconcile with his family. But when he gets out, he's frustrated by how little help there is for addicts. He wants to save the world but quickly realizes how broken the system is.

So, he turns to what he knows—selling drugs. But instead of profiting, he uses the money to help people get into recovery. It's a story that will raise all kinds of moral questions, and I think it could make for a compelling movie.

So, here I am, at seventy-three years old, still dreaming, still working, still chasing the next big thing. Maybe I'll die on a movie set, calling *action* one last time before jumping in front of the camera. That wouldn't be such a bad way to go.

But until then, I'm going to keep on pushing, keep on creating, and keep on dreaming.

For now, *Ciao Adios!*

*To Ending and New Beginnings!*